The Way of the Master

Seek and save the lost
the way Jesus did

Kirk Cameron   Ray Comfort

genesis
PUBLISHING GROUP

The Way of the Master
Basic Training Course Study Guide

Published by
Genesis Publishing Group
2002 Skyline Place
Bartlesville, OK 74006
www.genesis-group.net

ISBN 978-1-933591-01-8

Edited by Lynn Copeland

Design and production by Genesis Group

Cover photographs by Carol J. Scott, CJ Studio, Covina, CA (www.cj-studio.com)

Cartoons by Richard Gunther

Printed in the United States of America

Unless otherwise indicated, Scripture quotations are from the *New King James* version, © 1979, 1980, 1982 by Thomas Nelson Inc., Publishers, Nashville, Tennessee.

Scripture references marked KJV are from the *King James Version*.

Sixth printing, January 2011

Contents

Getting Started

Welcome to "The Way of the Master" Basic Training Course. Thank you for your concern for the lost! Sadly, evangelism is not a popular topic among many Christians, so we commend you for having the desire to learn to share your faith. For many who have implemented the principles of this course, sharing the gospel has become an exhilarating experience. As the name implies, this is basic training—simple and practical, with nothing complex and no big, heavy books to read. These basic principles are easy to learn, and the benefits will be very evident as you get into this course. You will discover there is no greater joy than to do God's will—seeking to save what is lost.

No doubt you have your fears and concerns when it comes to sharing your faith, but through the material presented here you will discover a newfound courage. Perhaps you have tried to share your faith and become discouraged or disillusioned by people's responses. Like countless others through the ages, you will find, as we both have, that using these biblical principles will revolutionize your life and witness. This is not some new method that we have devised, but is a timeless truth firmly rooted in the pages of Scripture, validated by centuries of church use, and proven by our own practice for over twenty-five years.

By following these principles, you will learn how to share your faith simply, effectively, biblically... the way Jesus did. This is accomplished primarily by addressing the sinner's conscience (the place of the knowledge of right and wrong), rather than the intellect (the place of argument). That means you don't have to be an expert in theology, archaeology, or Greek. You will never again need to feel intimidated by intellectuals, atheists, or the religious self-righteous. All you need is a desire to obey God . . . and to follow in the footsteps of Jesus.

Although this course can be used for individual study, it is ideally suited for use in small and large groups. Evangelism can seem fearful and intimidating, and a group setting can provide the needed encouragement and accountability.

For group use, notes for the leader are highlighted in the lessons, and additional Leader's Helps are available on page 114. Be sure to review these in planning the study and preordering materials.

Included in the course are CDs containing the audio portion of the videos. These are useful for the leader to gain further preparation, participants who miss viewing the video in the group meeting, or anyone who wants to hear it again as a refresher.

HOW TO USE THIS COURSE

Each lesson includes a video segment, classroom activities to help apply the teaching, homework assignments, and at-home Bible study. The video sessions vary from 30 to 50 minutes, but average 35 minutes in length. To allow adequate time for all the suggested activities, the recommended time for each weekly session is approximately an hour and a half.

Each lesson includes the following parts:

- **Open in Prayer:** Begin each lesson in prayer, asking God to give you a deeper understanding of His Word, particularly in the area of evangelism, and to give you a genuine concern for the lost.

- **Share Your Experiences:** As you put these principles into practice each week, hearing one another's experiences will spur you on, as you see that witnessing is not as fearful or difficult as you expected. Be sure to allow adequate time for this important interaction.

- **Point to Ponder:** Quietly read this thought-provoking text before viewing the video, to prepare your heart for the class.

- **View the Video:** Watch the video as a group, pausing where indicated for an activity.

- **Apply the Principles:** This section contains discussion and role-play activities to help you apply the principles taught in the video to your life. Depending on your group size, you may want to divide into smaller groups to discuss the questions. Allow each participant to express his thoughts, being careful to avoid arguing or having anyone dominate the conversation. Focus on the questions or activities presented, and keep the session moving forward so you can get through the material in the available time. With a limited class time, try to go through the main questions listed. For those who can accommodate a longer group time, additional discussion questions are given in the text.

- **Quality Quote:** These pearls of wisdom, gleaned from evangelistic giants such as Charles Spurgeon, will help you focus on our sober responsibility to reach the lost. Bring each quote to life by having someone stand and proclaim it to the group. Don't just "read" it, but strive to reenact history by "preaching" it as though you were speaking to a congregation as the author himself!

- **Preacher's Progress:** "Eavesdrop" on these helpful witnessing conversations, written in the style of *Pilgrim's Progress* by John Bunyan. To make these more meaningful, perform them as a skit, with the leader playing the part of "Christian" and a confident volunteer playing the other character ("Tim Burr," etc.). Assign these roles beforehand so the individuals can review the material and really put themselves into the role.

  "Set the stage" by arranging a couple of chairs (or other props), announce the characters' names, and describe the setting for that scene. Have fun with this as you act it out for the group.

- **Close in Prayer:** This will end the group time for this lesson. Be sure to pray for each other throughout the course, that no distractions would keep anyone from completing it. (It *will* be a battle!)

- **Break Out of Your Comfort Zone:** These weekly assignments are the most important part of the course. We are to be *doers* of the Word, not hearers only. Each consists of two parts: an "At-Home Preparation" and a "Real-World Application." Every week you will be challenged to stretch your evangelistic muscles, interact with others, and share what you have learned with the lost in your community. This gentle, gradual process is designed to help you feel comfortable and confident as you learn to share your faith.

To receive the maximum benefit from the course, you *must* commit to completing these activities. They are easy and don't require much time, but are crucial in easing you out of your comfort zone. In addition, you will be expected to share these experiences with others during the next session.

- **For Deeper Study:** While completing this Bible study portion of the homework is not essential to enjoy this course, we highly recommend that you do as much as possible. God's Word is powerful, and in searching it you will discover wonderful truths that reinforce what you're learning in class.

- **Memory Verse:** At the end of each homework assignment is a memory verse. Rather than the typical memory verses, which are designed to comfort the Christian, these are for use in witnessing to bring biblical truths to the lost.

- **Words of Encouragement:** These letters from others who have discovered "The Way of the Master" will encourage you to persevere as you learn the joy of sharing the gospel. They may also give you ideas on how to implement the principles you are learning through this study.

A RADICAL IDEA

Whether you're leading this course in a home study, Sunday school period, or discipleship training class, your desire will be to stick with the schedule and stay within the allotted timeframe for this study. However, the goal of this course is not simply to have people complete its eight lessons, but to transform the lives of each of the participants. Therefore, we propose a radical idea: Take whatever time is needed to ensure that these principles sink in and are then lived out. The souls of the lost are far too valuable to do otherwise.

For example, if after Lesson 3 you find that only 20 percent of participants were bold enough (or concerned enough) to even leave a tract on the ground, we strongly urge you not to continue to Lesson 4.

The homework assignments are progressive, and their gradual design is intended to be doable by even the most timid among us. If participants are not doing the first step, they will not take the next one.

Instead, we suggest you spend that week's group time in re-viewing the previous week's video, discussing its principles, praying for boldness, pondering the fate of the lost, and role-playing that activity—whatever you feel is needed—until participants become comfortable at that step. It may take twelve weeks to go through the eight-lesson course, but the result will be that participants will actually implement the material. Again, the goal is not simply to get through the study, but to transform the participants into confident witnesses for Jesus Christ.

With mutual encouragement and accountability from the group, trusting in the Lord to help you, you can do it. May God richly bless you as you take this journey into the often forgotten world of normal, *biblical* evangelism.

KIRK CAMERON
RAY COMFORT

LESSON 1
Cultivating Compassion for the Lost

▶ *Materials Needed: Paper, pen, and envelope for each participant*
Leader's Note: Begin the class by briefly sharing a little about yourself and why you're leading this course.

OPEN IN PRAYER

SHARE YOUR EXPERIENCES

As time allows, go around the room and, one at a time, stand and briefly share why you have come to this class. What are you hoping to accomplish by taking this course? Do you want to overcome your fear of sharing your faith or simply fine-tune your evangelism skills? Are you here because you have a concern for someone's salvation, or because you want to develop a concern?

POINT TO PONDER

Think of the frightening story Jesus told in Luke 16 about Lazarus and the rich man. Some believe this was simply a parable, but Jesus began by saying "There was," and He spoke of Lazarus by name. So it would seem that there really was a man named Lazarus and there really was a rich man who ended up in the torments of a very real hell. This should motivate us to cry out in prayer for the lost and then desperately do all we can with God's help to reach them. The sad irony is that in hell the rich man, who let a beggar starve at his gate, suddenly developed a concern for the fate of his unsaved family. His stony heart finally found compassion, and it was the reality of the fires of hell that changed him. Unfortunately, it was too late for him to put compassion into action, but it's not too late for us. In light of the reality of hell, we can have compassion for those we care about. This video segment is designed to steer us toward an empathy that will compel us to reach out to the unsaved.

As you watch the video, pay careful attention to the heartbreaking story of the firefighter and be sure to make a judgment about what his punishment should be.

VIEW THE VIDEO Cultivating Compassion for the Lost (30 minutes)

Apply the Principles

1. Who are the people whose salvation you are most concerned about? What are you doing about it?

2. With whom do you find it more difficult to share the gospel: family and friends, or complete strangers? Why?

▶ *Leader's Note: Hand out paper, pens, and envelopes to participants.*

3. Write a letter to God. Say something like, "God, these are my hopes and desires for this course. This is what I'm afraid of and this is what I'm hoping You'll do in me." Then write out what you want to see God do in your life through these lessons. Seal it in an envelope and place your name on it. No one is going to read it. Give it to the leader for safekeeping. It will be returned to you at the end of the course, and you will then see how God answered your prayers. Be sure to do this because it will be a very meaningful experience when you graduate.

► Leader's Note: If you have a longer class time, you may want to discuss the following additional questions.

4. How did you react as you heard the firefighter's story? What did the firefighter do that was wrong?

5. Can you think of any justification for his lack of concern? Was the fire chief justified in dishonorably discharging him from the fire department? What sentence did *you* give the firefighter?

6. How would you describe your current attitude about the fate of the lost: a) unconcerned; b) concerned; c) alarmed; d) horrified?

7. Did you find it helpful to see someone on the program witnessing? Why or why not?

QUALITY QUOTE

► *Leader's Note: Remember, for maximum impact, don't just read this, preach it! Go on, be Charles Spurgeon!*

The saving of souls, if a man has once gained love to perishing sinners and his blessed master, will be an all-absorbing passion to him. It will so carry him away, that he will almost forget himself in the saving of others. He will be like the brave fireman, who cares not for the scorch or the heat, so that he may rescue the poor creature on whom true humanity has set its heart. If sinners will be damned, at least let them leap to hell over our bodies. And if they will perish, let them perish with our arms about their knees, imploring them to stay. If hell must be filled, at least let it be filled in the teeth of our exertions, and let not one go there unwarned and unprayed for.
—*Charles Spurgeon*

PREACHER'S PROGRESS

The characters: Christian and Mrs. Smith
Scene setting: Christian goes to his friend Erik's workplace, and greets the receptionist, Mrs. Smith.

Christian: "Hi, Mrs. Smith. How are you doing? I'm here to see Erik."

Mrs. Smith: "Are you two having lunch again? I haven't seen him come through the lobby today. He came into work last week with a bad hangover. Probably the same thing has happened today. How was church?"

Christian: "It was really good. We had Brother Don Waterdowns come in and do a series of miracle meetings. Hundreds gave their hearts to the Lord. I'm in charge of the follow-up program. Man, I didn't realize how easy it is to get people saved! Lots were getting blessed and people were coming to the altar without even being preached to."

Mrs. Smith: "What a blessing. We had him at our church too. He advocates 'non-confrontational friendship evangelism.'"

Christian: "Yes. I like that. It's what I've been using with Erik. We've become good buddies over the years."

Mrs. Smith: "I like that approach too. It's so much better than shoving the gospel down people's throats."

Christian: "True. That can alienate them. I'm waiting for the right time to bring up the subject of God with Erik. It's been two years now. I don't want to make him feel uncomfortable. Erik came to one of the meetings, and he really seemed to enjoy it. That's the good thing about non-confrontational evangelism. Maybe today he will bring up the subject. I never do, because I don't want to offend him. I'm just a good friend, and I think that's the right approach."

Mrs. Smith: "I agree. I'll call his secretary. Perhaps she will know why he's late."

Christian: "Okay. Thanks."

Mrs. Smith: "Jeannie, Rose Smith here. Is Erik in? Christian Loveless is here to see … "

Christian: "What's wrong? Your face has turned pale!"

Mrs. Smith: "I … I'm afraid Erik died during the night. He had an aneurysm in his sleep and was pronounced dead at 8:17 this morning…"

Friendship evangelism that doesn't seek a way to quickly tell people about their eternal fate is the ultimate betrayal of trust. How can we call ourselves a friend of someone we don't bother to warn of terrible danger? Friends don't let friends go to hell.

▶ *Leader's Note: Review the "Break Out of Your Comfort Zone" assignments with the group, and challenge participants to invest the necessary time to complete the homework activities.*

CLOSE IN PRAYER

Break Out of Your Comfort Zone

This portion of the homework is not optional. To receive the maximum benefit from this course, you *must* commit to completing the "Break Out of Your Comfort Zone" activities. The at-home assignment will prepare you for taking the next step—applying what you're learning in the real world. They're not tough or time-consuming, but are very important in easing you out of your comfort zone. You will also be expected to share your experiences during the next session.

1. *At-Home Preparation:* Imagine that you are sound asleep in bed, and your house is on fire. There's a fire station next door. What virtues would you want the firefighters to have? Write them down

(alertness, training, courage, concern for others, etc.). Ask yourself whether you have those necessary virtues as a Christian. Indicate which ones you think you possess and which you need to work on.

2. *Real-World Application:* Call two people from your church and say, "I'm taking an evangelism course called 'The Way of the Master,' and as part of the homework, I need to ask someone a few questions. Can you help me with this?" Then ask the following questions:

- Do you share your faith regularly? *(Many people feel they "share their faith" if they mention God or church, so ask what they mean.)* Do you go out of your way to verbally share the gospel with strangers?
- What is the main reason you don't share your faith more often?

Write down their answers and bring them to the next session.

For Deeper Study

While completing this section of the homework is not essential to enjoy this course, we highly recommend that you do as much as possible. God's Word is powerful and in searching it you will discover wonderful truths that reinforce what you're learning in class.

1. Read Jeremiah 1:5–10. Do you think that God's intimate knowledge of Jeremiah (verse 5) was confined to him, or do you think God has this same knowledge of all of us (see Psalm 139)?

2. What was Jeremiah's response to the knowledge that God had set him apart for His purposes (verse 6)?

3. What was the real reason underlying Jeremiah's excuse (verse 8)?

Words of Encouragement

I have been studying the Way of the Master now for 3 weeks and have seen God work in miraculous ways! I could hardly wait to go to the train station to begin sharing the gospel with people. That very first day, the second person I spoke with, a girl in her early twenties, accepted Christ!

That was 2½ weeks ago, and I have shared Christ now with 20–30 people. Just yesterday, while picking up a suit from the tailor, I was contemplating sharing the gospel with her. She is Vietnamese, her husband is Buddhist, and her son is Catholic. As I thought about witnessing to her, she asked, "What church you believe?" Talk about an ice-breaker! I spoke with her for 45 minutes and she accepted Christ! As I was praying for her at the end, a customer walked into her shop. I began to wrap up my prayer and fully expected, after finishing, to see her head lifted and eyes open, greeting the customer and letting him know that she would be right with him. Instead, when I opened my eyes, she was still in prayer with her head bowed, her eyes closed, and her little hands clasped together!

She was so happy and full of joy as I left! She could not thank me enough! She just kept saying, "Thankyouson! Thankyouson!" How this made me praise God! It also helped me to see that God often does the ice-breaking when we are prepared and available for Him to use!

I can't thank you enough for your ministry. This biblical method of evangelism has revolutionized my service to God, my perspective of His holiness, and my love and compassion for people. There is nothing more urgent, important, or exhilarating than being used by Him in this way: calling others to repentance and to Him. —*Pastor Victor H., Texas*

4. What is your initial reaction to the thought that God wants to use you to reach the lost? If you are fearful, what do you fear?

5. What assurances does God give Jeremiah in these verses?

6. Read Exodus 3:11 and 4:10. What excuses did Moses give when God wanted to use him?

What assurances did God give him (see 3:12 and 4:11,12)?

7. When God called Gideon, what was his excuse (see Judges 6:15)?

Read Judges 6:25–27. Why did Gideon do what God wanted him to do at night?

8. What assurances did God give Gideon (vv. 14,16)?

9. Read 1 Corinthians 2:1–5. How did Paul feel when he preached?

Can you identify with Paul? Why do you think he did it anyway?

10. According to verses 4,5, why would God call such unqualified people as Paul, Jeremiah, Moses, Gideon,... and you?

11. Read and explain these verses in your own words: Proverbs 29:25; Deuteronomy 31:6; Isaiah 41:10.

Read Philippians 4:13, and explain the meaning of the word "all."

In light of God's promises to be with you and help you, and in light of His love expressed to you on the cross, can you think of any legitimate excuse for not being a true and faithful witness of Jesus Christ? List here. ➜ ☐

MEMORY VERSE

"It is appointed for men to die once,
but after this the judgment..."
HEBREWS 9:27

LESSON 2
Discovering Hell's Best Kept Secret

OPEN IN PRAYER

SHARE YOUR EXPERIENCES

Briefly share the results of the previous session's "Break Out of Your Comfort Zone" assignment. You asked two Christian friends, "Do you share your faith regularly? If not, what's the main reason you don't?"

POINT TO PONDER

Do you remember your thoughts after watching the "Firefighter" segment? We hope you were appalled that any human being could stand by and allow someone to perish. Such a thought should horrify us. And yet most believers today are not horrified at the thought that lost people all around them are perishing. So strive to always keep that sense of compassion uppermost in your mind, because it will greatly motivate you to witness. The fuel that drives us to share the gospel should be our gratitude to God for the cross, combined with a deep concern for the terrible fate of unbelievers.

Think of those you know who are not saved—your family, close friends, coworkers, fellow students, next-door neighbors. Without the blood of the Savior, those you are thinking of will one day be cast into the Lake of Fire. We should be utterly dismayed at the thought of that happening to *anyone*.

If we are lacking the fuels of compassion for others and gratitude for our own salvation, the task of sharing our faith will become a chore, seeming like a loathsome obligation. If our vehicle runs out of fuel, we'll have to push it rather than drive it. In the same way, if we have to push the vehicle of evangelism, it will be a tiresome task, while driving it will be exhilarating. Without the gas of gratitude, our attitude won't be an enthusiastic "I delight to do Your will," but a begrudging "I *have* to do Your will."

What each of us needs is a Garden of Gethsemane experience, where we lay down our own will and yield ourselves once and for all to the will of God. It was in a garden where Adam first said to God, "Not Your will, but *mine* be done," and it's in a garden where we need to say, "Not my will, but Yours be done."

When Jesus dropped to His knees in agonizing prayer, His disciples were unconcerned with reality. They were in a dream world. Don't be discouraged that the rest of the professing Church is asleep when it comes to seeking the lost. Instead, find a quiet place, get on your knees and say, "Father, the thought of sharing the gospel with strangers and my loved ones makes me sweat great drops of blood in fear. Yet not my will, but Yours be done." Make it so real that the next time you're standing next to a stranger at the grocery store or chatting with someone you care about, you will remember your Gethsemane experience.

Before we continue, take a moment right now for silent prayer as you meditate on the cross and surrender yourself completely to the Lord. This is a very necessary step. We are about to lay a very important foundation in this course.

VIEW THE VIDEO Discovering Hell's Best Kept Secret (38 minutes)

► *Leader's Note: Encourage participants to reflect on their own relationship with the Lord. Be aware that some people will feel conviction after watching this video, realizing that something is wrong in their walk with God. Invite the group to have a time for quiet reflection to "examine [themselves] as to whether [they] are in the faith" (2 Corinthians 13:5). After several minutes, offer a prayer on behalf of all the participants, thanking God for His grace and clear instructions in Scripture to come to Jesus, not for "life enhancement," but with a full surrender to the Savior.*

Apply the Principles

1. Why would an individual's understanding of his specific, personal violations of God's Law help the good news of the gospel to make more sense?

2. According to Romans 3:19, what is one function of God's Law? Why is this function so important?

3. What was the primary reason you came to the Savior? Did you have a thorough knowledge of your sin? Where did that knowledge come from? Did you have a fear of God?

► *Leader's Note: If you have a longer class time, you may want to discuss the following additional questions.*

4. Since we are saved only by grace, through faith, and not by the Law, what then is the primary purpose of God's Law for the sinner? (See Galatians 3:24.)

5. Do you think some people make a "decision for Christ" out of a wrong motive? Why or why not? Does the person witnessing have a responsibility to clearly communicate the right (biblical) motive? What should that motive be?

6. Explain the concept of "Law to the proud, grace to the humble."

7. How does the Law reveal to us our true state? Explain the dust analogy in your own words.

► *Leader's Note: Have someone stand up and preach this like Truth is going out of style... because it is!*

"I do not believe that any man can preach the gospel who does not preach the Law... Lower the Law and you dim the light by which man perceives his guilt. This is a very serious loss to the sinner rather than a gain, for it lessens the likelihood of his conviction and conversion. I say you have deprived the gospel of its ablest auxiliary [its most powerful weapon] when you have set aside the Law. You have taken away from it the schoolmaster that is to bring men to Christ ... They will never accept grace till they tremble before a just and holy Law. Therefore the Law serves a most necessary purpose, and it must not be removed from its place."
—*Charles Spurgeon*

PREACHER'S PROGRESS

The characters: Christian and Al Cohol
Scene setting: Two guys standing outside the workplace during a coffee break

Christian: "Hi, Al. How are you doing?"

Al Cohol: "Awful!"

Christian: "Why's that?"

Al Cohol: "I've got troubles."

Christian: "What sort of troubles?"

Al Cohol: "Big troubles. My wife left me."

Christian: "I'm sorry to hear that. What happened?"

Al Cohol: "Well, I've got a little problem with alcohol... and a bit of a gambling problem. They're no big deal. Mind if I smoke?"

Christian: "Go ahead."

Al Cohol: "Hey, can you lend me a couple of dollars? I smashed my car up the other day and need to get it fixed."

Christian: "How did that happen?"

Al Cohol: "I'd had a couple of beers and was on my way to court to pay a speeding fine—third DUI this month. What a pain! Would you believe it? I parked in a red zone and got another ticket while I was in court. Stupid cops."

Christian: "Do you ever pray?"

Al Cohol: "All the time. I told you, I have problems."

Christian: "What do you think happens after someone dies—where do they go?"

Al Cohol: "Heaven."

Christian: "Everyone?"

Al Cohol: "Yep. Everyone."

Christian: "So, do you think that you'll go there?"

Al Cohol: "Of course."

Christian: "Why?"

Al Cohol: "Because I'm a good person."

Christian: "Have you kept the Ten Commandments?" (Christian goes through the Commandments, then into the gospel.)

Al Cohol: "I know I'm guilty, and I know that if I died tonight I would go to hell, but I've got all these problems I have to work out before I get into that stuff."

Christian: "Listen to me, Al. All these problems combined a thousand times over won't be anything like the problem you'll have on Judgment Day if you don't turn from your sin and trust Jesus Christ. You may not see this now, but I care enough about you to tell you the truth.

I don't want you to go to hell, *you* don't want to go to hell, and *God* doesn't want you to go to hell. Please don't shrug this off, Al. There is nothing more important than your eternal salvation. Does that make sense?"

Al Cohol: "Yah, it does. Hey, thanks for the talk."

The modern gospel gives the wrong solution for the wrong problem. Here's an analogy to illustrate how important it is that we address sin, and not the sinner's everyday problems. A child was once running through a wooded area when he fell onto a sharp stick and cut his jugular vein. His father immediately scooped him up, held his thumb on the child's bleeding neck and rushed him to the hospital.

As they burst into the emergency room and a doctor approached them, the small boy lifted his hand. When he fell, a tiny splinter had penetrated his thumb and he wanted the doctor to take it out. Of course, the good doctor ignored the child's plea, and immediately began work to stop the life-threatening injury to his neck.

In their ignorance, many Christians preach a message that causes the sinner to hold up his splintered thumb to God, rather than that which is truly life-threatening. They tell the world that Jesus will fix the splinter of a bad marriage, drug addiction, alcoholism, loneliness, etc., when the real reason a sinner should come to the Savior is that his life's blood is draining from his neck. God, the Great Physician, is most concerned with addressing the fatal wound of sin.

CLOSE IN PRAYER

Break Out of Your Comfort Zone

1. *At-Home Preparation:* Go back in your mind to your conversion experience, and try to recall the thoughts of that day. What do you think was your greatest sin? Was there a knowledge of future pun-

ishment? Think of what would have happened to you if you had died in your sins. Then write out a prayer expressing your gratitude to God for the cross.

2. *Real-World Application:* Perhaps you don't have an outgoing personality. If you prefer to keep to yourself, ask God to help you change that, for the sake of the lost. A firefighter may be the personality type that likes to stay alone in the comfort of a firetruck and read books, but if he wants to do what he knows he should, he must change that attitude. So, as a first step out of the "truck," make the effort this week to practice being friendly and greeting complete strangers each day until the next session. When you walk into the grocery store, the gas station, school, or work, give a friendly greeting to people you don't know. (Of course, be friendly with those you do know, too!) If you don't normally rub shoulders with strangers, go somewhere where you can.

It may seem difficult at first to greet a complete stranger, but force yourself to say, "Hi. How are you doing?" Try it and you will see that it really isn't difficult at all. In fact, it will almost certainly bring smiles to people's faces and make you feel good yourself. But remember that you will have to take the initiative. Strive to greet at least ten strangers before the next session. Although this may seem awkward, it's a very important step toward sharing your faith.

For Deeper Study

1. What is the biblical definition of sin (see 1 John 3:4)?

2. What is it that will cause a sinner to agree with our message? (See Romans 2:15,21,22.)

3. Charles Spurgeon warned, "I do not believe that any man can preach the gospel who does not preach the Law. The Law is the needle, and you cannot draw the silken thread of the gospel through a man's heart unless you first send the needle of the Law to make way for it." Explain what a needle does for thread, and then what the Law does for the gospel (see Romans 5:20; 7:13).

4. In his book *Holiness*, J. C. Ryle wrote, "Let us expound and beat out the Ten Commandments, and show the length, and breadth, and depth, and height of their requirements. This is the way of our Lord in the Sermon on the Mount. We cannot do better than follow His plan." In Matthew 5:21–37, note where Jesus "beat out the Ten Commandments."

5. Study Matthew 15:19,20 and identify each Commandment to which Jesus refers.

Words of Encouragement

I recently returned from Brazil where I shared the gospel with many people. I started with creation, telling them that God created them and everything they see, but that man rebelled against God. I told them God gave His Law to show us that we have sinned against Him, then I went through the Ten Commandments one by one. In almost every home I preached in, the people were somewhat unconcerned until I went through the Law. It was so incredible.

The guys who were with me noticed the same thing. They saw the "deer in the headlights" look on people's faces when I brought out the Law. They realized why I shared the Ten Commandments before I could explain it. They knew, simply because of the reaction of the people when I got to that point in the message. What a testimony to the conviction of the Holy Spirit through the Law.

Only two people (out of about 50–70) rejected the gospel during the week I was there. The first home I preached in, one couple broke down crying when I went through the Law. The woman was a witch, but she came to Christ. Another lady who was studying at the Seventh Day Adventist church broke down crying when I continued to press her, "Why would God let you, a sinner, into heaven on the Day of Judgment?" She yielded her life to Christ. Jehovah's Witnesses who came to Christ set up meetings with their friends within two days because they wanted their friends to hear the gospel presented to them. It was incredible. —Ky F., Louisiana

Do the same thing with Mark 10:17–22.

6. Read Romans 7:7. How did Paul gain an understanding of the true nature of sin?

Based on Paul's statement (and 1 John 3:4), is there any way people can know they have sinned against God, other than by the Law?

Some people think that sinners have an inherent understanding of their sin and therefore don't need the Law. What do Ephesians 4:18 and Romans 3:11 tell us about the understanding of the lost?

7. Romans 3:23 says, "All have sinned and fall short of the glory of God." To know what standard Paul was referring to when he said "the glory of God," we need to understand the context of verse 23. Read verses 19–31; what subject did Paul say was "established" (or "upheld")?

For another clue, let's look at 2 Corinthians 3:7. What does Scripture say is "glorious" ("came with glory") that was engraved on stones?

Based on these answers, what then is the standard from which we all fall short ("the glory of God")?

8. When we use Romans 3:23 in witnessing, why should we be sure to specify that it is *the Law* from which we all fall short? What effect do you think it has on the lost when we fail to do so?

MEMORY VERSE

"You have heard that it was said to those of old, 'You shall not commit adultery.' But I say to you that whoever looks at a woman to lust for her has already committed adultery with her in his heart."

MATTHEW 5:27,28

LESSON 3
Learning to Overcome Fear

► *Materials Needed: At least five Ice Breakers for each partici-*
pant. In addition to those included in the course, a large selec-
tion of unique tracts can be found at WayoftheMaster.com.
The greater the variety of tracts available in class, the more
enjoyable the demonstration will be.

OPEN IN PRAYER

SHARE YOUR EXPERIENCES

Think of a time when you sensed that you should have
shared the gospel with someone but didn't. Why didn't you?
Assemble into groups of two or three and briefly discuss
your experiences. Then share the results of the previous
session's "Break Out of Your Comfort Zone" assignment.
Was it as difficult as you thought it would be to greet
strangers this past week? Were you fearful, or did you have
negative thoughts just before you did it?

POINT TO PONDER

Most of us are familiar with the concept known as "friendship evangelism." This is the idea that we should befriend
someone and build a relationship with the person *before*
we witness to him. But *how long* should we develop the
relationship before we talk to him about God?

As we have considered previously, what will happen to your lost friend if he dies while you are taking the time to build a relationship? There is no nice way to say it: he will go to hell for eternity if he dies without the Savior. He will end up in the Lake of Fire, so how can you even consider taking that risk by letting too much time pass?

Here is an interesting thought about friendship evangelism. Who are the hardest people to witness to? Isn't it our unsaved relatives? Why is this? Perhaps it's because if you witness to someone with whom you have a good relationship, and offend him, you risk losing that relationship. But if you witness to a stranger and you offend him, you haven't lost anything at all.

So, make it easier for yourself: learn to witness to strangers. Make it a way of life to share the gospel with people you don't know. This will help encourage you to be bold. Understand that you can develop a rapport and build a "relationship" with someone in three or four minutes, if you care about the person's salvation. Once the door is open, then share the truth, knowing that the person to whom you are speaking may not have tomorrow.

VIEW THE VIDEO Learning to Overcome Fear, Part 1 (13 minutes)

▶ *Leader's Note: Pause after viewing Part 1 of the video. Hand out the Ice Breakers that have been provided with the course (IQ Test, $1 Million Bill, Curved Illusion), as well as any additional tracts that you may have ordered. Make sure participants have one of each for in-class use, and several of the IQ Test and $1 Million Bills for their homework assignment.*

Apply the Principles

Now we're going to have fun with a role-play in a safe environment. Break into pairs (preferably same-sex). Take a few minutes to practice giving each Ice Breaker to your "non-Christian" partner so you can begin to get comfortable using these new tools. There's no pressure to share the gospel at this point.

Here are some suggested phrases that can be used when passing out tracts:

- "Did you get one of these?" (any Ice Breaker)
- "You're doing a great job today. Keep the change." "I appreciate what you're doing. Thanks a million!" ($1 Million Bill)
- "Do you like optical illusions? Watch this!" (pink and blue Curved Illusion)
- "Do you like IQ tests? Try this one!" (IQ Test)

▶ *Leader's Note: Play Part 2 of the video, instructing participants to pay attention to the last witnessing conversation. Note the way Ray first addresses the man's intellect, then his conscience.*

VIEW THE VIDEO Learning to Overcome Fear, Part 2 (25 minutes)

After the video, read the following encouraging letter, which was written by the young man shown in the video:

> Hello, my name is Ryan and I was interviewed over a year ago by Ray Comfort at California State University Long Beach. Since then I have been approached several times by people that saw me on "The Way of the Master." I've been told that I am presented on some specific episode for several minutes. I would like to view this episode in order to satisfy my personal curiosity and to observe what context my footage was orchestrated. I recall conversing with
>
> Mr. Comfort for at least an hour and I think I made an impression on him. I am an atheist and am sure I was presented as such ... I have since changed my ways, and would like to have a reminder of that cold, dark place I once resided in so comfortably. I appreciate your anticipated response.

Keep in mind, whenever you are fearful about sharing your faith, that you can have an eternal impact on people. Taking the time to share the gospel will plant seeds in their hearts, leading them toward the truth.

Break into small groups and discuss the following questions:

1. What experiences have you had (that you can openly talk about) where your conscience has strongly spoken to you?

2. How can you appeal directly to the human conscience as you speak to sinners about their salvation?

▶ *Leader's Note: If you have a longer class time, you may want to discuss the following additional questions.*

3. How would you describe the human conscience?

4. What does the word "conscience" mean?

5. How carefully did you listen to the voice of your conscience before your conversion? What is your attitude toward its voice now?

6. How is man at war against God? What Bible verse tells us that we have a God-given "ally" in the battle for souls?

QUALITY QUOTE

▶ *Leader's Note: You are in 19th century England. The crowd is hanging on your every word. Go on, preach it!*

People will never set their faces decidedly towards heaven, and live like pilgrims, until they really feel that they are in danger of hell ... Let us expound and beat out the Ten Commandments, and show the length, and breadth, and depth, and height of their requirements. This is the way of our Lord in the Sermon on the Mount. We cannot do better than follow His plan. We may depend on it: men will never come to Jesus, and stay with Jesus, and live for Jesus, unless they really know why they are to come, and what is their need. Those whom the Spirit draws to Jesus are those whom the Spirit has convinced of sin. Without thorough conviction of sin, men may seem to come to Jesus and follow Him for a season, but they will soon fall away and return to the world.

—*J. C. Ryle*

PREACHER'S PROGRESS

The characters: Christian and Robin Banks
Scene setting: A park bench during lunchtime

Christian: "Hi. How are you doing?"

Robin Banks: "Fine. How are you?"

Christian: "Good, thanks. Mind if I ask a question? Do you know of any good churches in this area?"

Robin Banks: "I don't know. I haven't been to church for years."

Christian: "Do you have a Christian background?"

Robin Banks: "Yes. I went to Sunday school, but grew out of it when I got older."

Christian: "By the way, my name's Christian. What's yours?"

Robin Banks: "Robin Banks."

Christian: "Nice to meet you, Robin. Would you consider yourself to be a good person...I mean, do you think you've kept the Ten Commandments?"

Robin Banks: "Pretty much."

Christian: "Have you ever told a lie?"

Robin Banks: "Yes."

Christian: "What does that make you?"

Robin Banks: "A liar."

Christian: "Have you ever stolen something?"

Robin Banks: "I know what you're doing. You're laying a guilt trip on me."

Christian: "Really? Which Commandment makes you feel guilty—'You shall not lie'?"

Robin Banks: "No."

Christian: "You shall not steal?"

Robin Banks: "Um . . . I really don't want to talk about this anymore."

Christian: "I'm sorry. I didn't mean to offend you. What do you do for a living, Robin?"

Robin Banks: "I . . . um . . . I work in a bank. I've got to go now . . ."

Never be discouraged if someone suddenly wants to end a conversation. If the person feels guilty as you go through the Commandments, it's probably because he is guilty. The Law has that effect on sinners. You may not be aware of the fear and concern that grips the heart of someone you are witnessing to, but agitation or frustration is a good sign that something is going on in the heart.

▶ *Leader's Note: Review the "Break Out of Your Comfort Zone" assignments with the group, and commit together to completing them before the next session. Engaging in these activities is absolutely critical for participants to experience the growth they are looking for. Encourage them not to chicken out!*

CLOSE IN PRAYER

Break Out of Your Comfort Zone

1. *At-Home Preparation:* Stand in front of a mirror. Make sure no one is around or can hear you. Look directly at your image and ask a friendly, "How are you doing?" Of course, you are going to feel a little foolish, but no one is watching except God. Then ask, "Did you get one of these?" Offer your reflection a tract, saying, "It's a gospel tract. Do you have a Christian background?" Then inquire, "What do you think happens after someone dies? Do you believe in heaven and hell?"

   Continue asking these questions until you shake off any self-consciousness. Get used to the sound of your own voice. Remember, you're not a weirdo and you don't sound like one. You are a warm and friendly Christian who genuinely cares about people. Keep practicing saying these things until it feels natural. If you don't feel comfortable doing this, repeat it again and again until you do.

2. *Real-World Application:* Carry tracts with you as you go through the week, leaving tracts where people will find them. For example, the IQ Cards fit great in any credit card slot. Every time you go to a gas station, leave a tract in the credit card slot at the pump. The next person will have to take it out to put his credit card in, and will appreciate having something to read while he's filling his gas tank.

   Place one in the ATM machine before you leave. Every time you go to the grocery store, discreetly go down

WHERE TO LEAVE TRACTS

- At pay phones
- In shopping carts
- In clothes pockets in clothing stores
- In letters to loved ones
- With a generous tip
- On seats in restaurant lobbies
- With fast-food employees, cashiers, flight attendants, cab drivers, and gas station workers
- In restrooms and at rest areas
- On ATM machines and bank counters
- In envelopes with bill payments
- In elevators
- On hotel dressers for the maid
- On ice machines
- On newspaper racks
- In waiting rooms of doctors' offices and hospitals
- On seats at airports, subways, and bus stations
- In plane seat pockets
- Inside magazines
- In cabs
- In laundromats

the beer aisle, placing tracts in the top slot in beer cases. Leave a $1 Million Bill in the tube at the bank drive-through, and put one in the tip jar at Starbucks. Place $1 Million Bills sticking out of your shirt pocket, and people will ask you about them. How great to have lost people asking you for gospel tracts!

Then as you lay your head on your pillow at night, there will be a deep sense of satisfaction knowing that you're planting seeds that could result in someone finding everlasting life.

For Deeper Study

1. Acts 24:10–27 gives us insight into how Paul testified of his faith in Christ. Read this account, then study 2 Timothy 2:23–26. Consider the spirit in which Paul tells Timothy to relate to the unsaved. How does Paul exercise these virtues when speaking to Felix?

Have you ever become impatient and even angry when witnessing to someone? Why did this happen?

2. The Greek word used in Acts 24:16 for "strive" is *askeo*, which means "to take pains, endeavor, exercise by training or discipline." Compare a good conscience to a good coach. What qualities should a good coach have?

Words of Encouragement

After viewing "The Way of the Master" course, today I graduated from mere church attendee to ministry. I grabbed my sample pack of Bible tracts provided and headed for the local shopping mall. In the fashion taught by the Lord Jesus Christ Himself and passed on to me by Ray and Kirk, I approached no fewer than 17 people, four of whom were Marines. One girl was a professing Muslim. One man from Colombia was a theology student. For the theology student, it was his first realization that sin was a condition of the heart and not necessarily a commission of the flesh. I presented the perfect Law of God, the Ten Commandments, and let the Holy Spirit challenge and convict them.

As stated in the instructions, I bypassed the intellect and spoke straight to the conscience. My questions were pointed yet sincere. Not one person challenged me in argument. I was amazed at how intently they all listened and participated and answered the questions. I had a wonderful time doing this. Though the approach was soft, humorous, and jovial, the gravity of the subject was not lost on any. One teenage girl's face turned red and her eyes welled up with tears of conviction.

Praise the Lord for this course. I found my feet of faith. I was thrilled to be used by the Lord to present the truth to those Marines serving our country in this time of war against terrorism. Thank you! —*Darrel R., Texas*

Does your conscience ever speak to you about the sin of apathy regarding evangelism? What can you do to ensure that you don't have an offending conscience in this area?

3. Has there ever been a time when you chose not to listen to the voice of your conscience? How did that make you feel?

What impact did that feeling have on your relationship with God (on your prayer life, etc.)?

4. Explain the work of the conscience according to Romans 9:1 and 2 Corinthians 1:12.

5. When Felix heard Paul "concerning the faith in Christ," what did Paul talk to him about (see Acts 24:25)?

Do you think this is how most Christians witness? If not, why not?

Read John 16:7,8. How does the content of Paul's message assist the Holy Spirit in His work?

6. According to Romans 2:15, what did Felix's conscience do for him as he listened to Paul, and why did it speak in such a way?

7. Read 1 Corinthians 9:16–22. Read it the first time as the words of the apostle Paul, then read it again out loud as your personal prayer to God. Begin with "Dear Father," and end with "In Jesus' name I pray. Amen."

MEMORY VERSE

"Do you not know that the unrighteous will not inherit the kingdom of God? Do not be deceived. Neither fornicators, nor idolaters, nor adulterers, nor homosexuals, nor sodomites, nor thieves, nor covetous, nor drunkards, nor revilers, nor extortioners will inherit the kingdom of God."

1 CORINTHIANS 6:9,10

LESSON 4
Practicing What You Preach

▶ *Materials Needed: One Quick Reference Card and at least ten Ice Breakers for each participant*

OPEN IN PRAYER

SHARE YOUR EXPERIENCES

Gather in groups of two or three and share the results of the previous "Break Out of Your Comfort Zone" assignment. What were some of the places where you left gospel tracts? Did you actually hand a tract to anyone as you greeted strangers? If so, what happened? Did you get a sense of joy or accomplishment in doing this?

After several minutes of group discussion, have two or three people share their experiences with the class.

POINT TO PONDER

The Scriptures give us insight into our enemy. We are told that we don't wrestle against flesh and blood, but against spiritual forces (see Ephesians 6:12). That's either true or it isn't. Do you believe that demons (evil spirits) can bombard your mind with negative thoughts when it comes to seeking the lost? Or do you think that it is merely your own fears? If you believe that it is simply your mind, then you won't bother putting on the full armor of God as listed in Ephesians 6. But if you understand that we have a very real enemy, then you will recognize the need for a very real armor. As a Christian, you should believe this is true not only because the Bible says so, but also because you will daily experience the reality of a spiritual battle.

Despite this, most of us forget that the spiritual realm is *the source* of negative thoughts. For example, you may be having thoughts of quitting this course. Other things in your life will demand more of your time, leaving you with little or no time to complete the assignments or attend the sessions. Or someone you love and respect may say something to discourage you from the task of evangelism. This is normal, particularly when it comes to anything to do with reaching out to the lost.

Remember, one of Satan's most powerful weapons is fear. Fear will make you want to stop taking this course and retreat into the barracks. So expect him to try to discourage you. Think of that word: "dis-courage." Satan wants to rid you of your *courage*. Therefore, soldier of Christ, make sure you have a sensitive ear to subtle discouraging thoughts, and recognize their source. Continually remember your Gethsemane experience—where you laid down your will and said, "God, I want to do Your will in my life. And Your will is that none perish."

Determine to continue in this course despite the discouragement, so that you are fully equipped to do God's will. You may have given up on other training in the past— such as learning how to play golf, lose weight, etc.—but the eternal welfare of the lost is too important for you to even consider not completing this course.

VIEW THE VIDEO Practicing What You Preach, Part 1 (25 minutes)

▶ *Leader's Note: Hand out the Quick Reference Cards and at least ten Ice Breakers for each participant. Explain that this card is, in essence, the entire course in their hand. This card* will serve as a guide for participants to stay on track as together you learn to speak to the conscience and share the gospel biblically. Ask the group to read aloud with you each of the letters and what they stand for, on both sides of the card.

IMPORTANT: Don't lose this card! It will be your "guide" each week and your "training coach" once you've completed the Basic Training Course. Place it in your wallet so you'll always have it with you.

▶ *Leader's Note: Play Part 2 of the video, instructing participants to look for how the principles on the card are used in the witnessing conversation.*

VIEW THE VIDEO **Practicing What You Preach, Part 2 (8 minutes)**

Apply the Principles

1. What is a good "inoffensive" question to ask to discover a person's spiritual condition? Why is this an effective question?

2. If you ask someone if he thinks he is a good person, and he says that he is, what can you say to help him see himself in light of God's standards?

▶ *Leader's Note: Have participants break into pairs (preferably same-sex) for the following role-play using Ice Breakers.*

3. Practice using different Ice Breakers to start a conversation about the Lord. Hand one to your partner with a friendly, "Did you get one of these?" or "Did you see this?" Then explain what it is and (if applicable) how it works. After saying that it's a gospel tract, you could ask, "What do you think happens when a person dies? Do you think you'll go to heaven?" Then ask, "Would you consider yourself to be a good person?" Take turns so everyone has a chance to do this.

► *Leader's Note: If you have a longer class time, you may want to discuss the following additional questions.*

4. Do you think that well-written gospel tracts can help to make the transition into spiritual things? Do you use them? Why or why not?

5. How else could you (or do you) bring up the topic of spiritual things?

6. Explain the world's understanding of the word "good." Then explain God's definition of the word.

7. What two things should we be trusting in if we have biblically shared the gospel with an unsaved person?

QUALITY QUOTE

► *Leader's Note: Preach this one with passion and urgency. Your hearers need to be awakened from their spiritual slumber!*

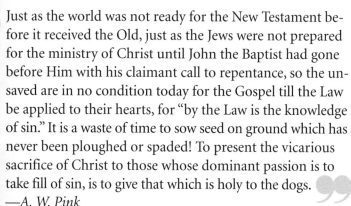

Just as the world was not ready for the New Testament before it received the Old, just as the Jews were not prepared for the ministry of Christ until John the Baptist had gone before Him with his claimant call to repentance, so the unsaved are in no condition today for the Gospel till the Law be applied to their hearts, for "by the Law is the knowledge of sin." It is a waste of time to sow seed on ground which has never been ploughed or spaded! To present the vicarious sacrifice of Christ to those whose dominant passion is to take fill of sin, is to give that which is holy to the dogs.
—A. W. Pink

PREACHER'S PROGRESS

*The characters: Christian and Tim Burr & Treesa Green
Scene setting: Christian and the tree-loving couple cross paths while hiking in a forest.*

Christian: "Hi, guys. How are you doing?"

Tim Burr: "We're fine."

Christian: "What are you doing here?"

Treesa Green: "Looking at trees. We love them."

Tim Burr: "We're here representing the eastside branch of TWIG."

Christian: "What's TWIG?"

Treesa Green: "'Trees Wherever I Go.' It's an organization that's grown a lot lately. We promise to take care of trees, wherever we go."

Christian: "That's commendable."

Tim Burr: "Thanks. We're putting down roots in this area."

Christian: "I agree, we should take care of trees, and we should be careful to use them for the purpose for which they're intended."

Treesa Green: "Right."

Christian: "Do you know what God made them for?"

Tim Burr: "We wouldn't actually say that *God* made trees. They evolved... over millions of years."

Christian: "Well, it seems kind of nice that we can use them to provide wood for warmth, housing, and furniture; make maple syrup for pancakes, rubber for tires, and a stack of other useful things; as well as turn the pulp into paper for books. We have trees that feed us with apples, peaches, bananas, apricots, etc. It's also a blessing that trees turn our carbon dioxide back into life-giving oxygen. We couldn't live without them."

Treesa Green: "Whatever. But that's our point. If we keep cutting down trees, there won't be any to give the air its oxygen. Trees are the lungs of the earth! It's an environmental crisis. We will all die. We *have* to prevent logging companies from cutting down the rain forests, or any trees for that matter!"

Christian: "So you want to protect trees. That's nice. Speaking of dying, I have a question for you. Do you know what is the number one killer of drivers in the U.S.?"

Tim Burr: "Drunk driving?"

Christian: "No. Trees."

Treesa Green: "Are you kidding?"

Christian: "No, I'm not actually. Lining the highways of America are millions of trees. When a car goes off a road and hits a tree, the tree doesn't move, the driver does—into eternity. In the late 1990s the state of Georgia spent $600 million to cut down all trees within 32 feet of the major highways to make them safer. A spokesman said 27 percent of all deaths each year in Georgia are from vehicles hitting trees on the side of the road. Can I ask you guys an important question?"

Tim Burr & Treesa Green: "Sure."

Christian: "What do you think happens when you die? Do you think that you will go to heaven?" (etc.)

CLOSE IN PRAYER

Break Out of Your Comfort Zone

1. *At-Home Preparation:* Practice "Shower Power"—As you shower each day, practice bringing up the subject of God. Don't worry about people hearing you; your family has probably heard you talking to yourself in the shower anyway. Here are a few suggestions to help you get started:

- "What do you think about all these hurricanes, earthquakes, and tsunamis? We never know when a tragedy may strike. Have you thought about what would happen to you if you died?"

- "What do you think of the 'Killer Bird Flu' in Asia? Scary, isn't it? Makes me think about how precious life is. What do you think happens when a person dies?"

- "Have you noticed how much we hear on the news about religion these days—religious movies, TV shows, celebrity beliefs, etc. Do you have a religious background?"

Thinking through several different ways to bring up the subject of God, and hearing yourself say them out loud, will help you feel much more comfortable and confident as you talk with people.

2. *Real-World Application:* Okay, get ready for sweaty palms. If you feel confident, as you continue to leave or give out tracts this week, warmly greet strangers then hand them your favorite Ice Breaker. Simply give it to the person the same way you did in class. You *can* do this! For example, when you're at the checkout stand, greet the cashier and give him a tract as you're leaving. Or as you're going through a fast-food drive-through, engage the person in a conversation about his job or his day. You want him to warm to you. Pass him a tract, say, "Please read this when you've got a minute," and then drop the pedal to the metal and drive away saying to yourself, "I did it! Thank you, Lord." Better to do it and run than to not do it at all. This may sound scary, but think of that person's eternal welfare. Then consider your worst-case scenario. You may hear, "No, thanks." If that happens, deal with it. It won't be pleasant to be rejected, but it isn't the end of the world. But more than likely, the person will take the tract, and even thank you for it.

Again, remember to smile and offer a warm greeting like, "Good morning. How are you doing?" Just the person's response will help dissipate your fears. Then when you ask, "Did you get one of these?" he will be more likely to respond positively because of your friendly greeting. And if someone asks what it is, be ready to just say, "It's a gospel tract" or "It has a gospel message on it. Please take the time to read it. Nice to meet you." If you hand out the $1 Million Bill, you may want to say, "It has a million-dollar question on the back. Be sure to read it!"

For Deeper Study

1. Read John 4:1–42. What does this passage show us about the priorities of the Son of God? (See Luke 15:4–7.)

2. What did Jesus say about the Samaritans and God (verse 22)?

   What does this tell us about the religions of the world? (See Acts 17:23; 1 Corinthians 10:20; and 2 John 9.)

3. In John 4:16–18, to which commandment was Jesus alluding as He spoke with the woman at the well? (See Romans 7:3.)

   According to verse 39, what was the result of her testifying?

   Based on this, how can we best imitate Jesus?

Words of Encouragement

Over the past few months our student ministry has been putting into practice the scriptural principles from the "Way of the Master" course. We started doing personal evangelism with family, friends and coworkers, then we slowly began witnessing to strangers in public places.

Our church is directly across the street from a junior high and half a block away from a high school. To share the gospel with larger groups of teenagers, we set up signs on our church lawn after school that invite people to take your IQ Test and win a prize. Then we do several public presentations of law and grace. During December we have signs that say "Have you been naughty or nice? Tell us what you think and win a prize!"

We've been able to share the gospel with up to 60 teens in half an hour. More and more students are hearing about sin, judgment, righteousness and the amazing grace of God through Jesus Christ. God has given us many opportunities to preach His message with clarity and boldness. We know that we are being faithful to the one and only gospel of Jesus Christ so any conversions will prayerfully be genuine. A lot of students have given some serious thought to their destiny without Christ.

Thanks for doing the work of evangelists and equipping this little church to preach for Christ. —*Joshua R., California*

4. Read Daniel 12:3. To what are we to "turn many"?

According to Proverbs 11:4, what delivers us from death?

5. What does the Holy Spirit convict the world of? (See John 16:8.)

What is the relationship among these items?

6. Why should we therefore mention the Law (see Romans 7:13)?

7. Matthew Henry said, "As that which is straight discovers that which is crooked, as the looking-glass shows us our natural face with all its spots and deformities, so there is no way of coming to that knowledge of sin which is necessary to repentance, and consequently to peace and pardon, but by comparing our hearts and lives with the Law." What is the link between the Law and repentance?

MEMORY VERSE

"Jesus answered and said to him, 'Most assuredly, I say to you, unless one is born again, he cannot see the kingdom of God.'"
JOHN 3:3

LESSON 5
Crafting the Message

▶ *Materials Needed: At least fifteen Ice Breakers for each person. Participants will need to have their Quick Reference Cards with them.*

OPEN IN PRAYER

SHARE YOUR EXPERIENCES

Briefly share the results of the previous "Break Out of Your Comfort Zone" assignment. What happened this past week when you handed someone a gospel tract? What was the person's reaction? Did it start a conversation about the Lord? Were you nervous before you did it? How did you feel afterward?

POINT TO PONDER

You've spent four weeks in this course so far. Have you had any exciting things happen regarding the sharing of your faith? How is your fear factor? Have you been able to resist discouraging thoughts? Always remember the positive side to the enemy's whisperings: fear can make you pray. This is a wonderful truth. Continually hearing the words "You can't do this" can deepen your trust in God. Of course you can't do it—without God's help. Let shaky knees put you on your knees. It's then that the negative of fear becomes the positive of prayer.

So don't let fear stop you in your tracks. Instead, let it remind you to rely on God's strength, wisdom, and ability. It was fear that drove Jesus to His knees in the Garden of

Gethsemane. Let fear bring you to your knees, then deny yourself, and unashamedly pick up the cross and follow Him who gave His life for you.

VIEW THE VIDEO Crafting the Message (35 minutes)

Apply the Principles

► *Leader's Note: Ask participants to take out their Quick Reference Cards and break into pairs (preferably same-sex, and different partners than in previous sessions).*

Discuss each question below and then role-play, using the Quick Reference Card as a guide, going through all the letters in WDJD and CRAFT. Help each other practice by having one partner play the part of the Christian and the other play a typical non-Christian. If role-playing is outside your comfort zone, try it anyway. It will help you overcome your fears in general, and that's what this course is all about.

1. What is the first steppingstone? What does that letter stand for? Take turns asking that question as the Christian and letting your "non-Christian" partner answer.

2. What is the second steppingstone? Ask your partner the "W" question again, and then follow it up with the "D" question: "Do you think you've kept the Ten Commandments?" This is not an offensive question because most people think that they are good and have more or less kept the Commandments.

3. Now open up the Commandments and ask the questions, "Have you ever told a lie?" "Have you ever stolen something?" "Have you ever looked with lust?" Remember, you're not judging anyone; you're just asking questions, like a doctor asking his patients questions to discover whether they have symptoms of a disease.

4. What is the third steppingstone? Ask your partner this question, being sure you allow plenty of time for the

answer. Urge the person to think carefully because it is such an important issue, and ask him to be honest.

5. What is the fourth steppingstone? Ask this question with a serious attitude. If the person says, "Hell," it shows that he sees his terrible plight. If he answers, "Heaven," help him see the error of his thinking by reminding him that he has already admitted to lying, stealing, adultery, etc. Explain that because God is good, it makes sense that He will punish sin (Revelation 21:8; 1 Corinthians 6:9,10; Romans 6:23), and hell is God's place of punishment.

6. When speaking with an unsaved person, what should you wait for before you share the "good news" of the gospel? What are you trying to detect in the person?

7. What do the letters CRAFT stand for? Practice using the CRAFT phrases, one by one, just as you did with WDJD. Remember, these phrases are simply a structure, not a script. Use them as you would training wheels while learning to ride a bike. Memorize the phrases during this course, and when you are confident, use your own words, inject your own personality, and be *yourself*.

IMPORTANT: Keep the Quick Reference Card with you at all times, reviewing it daily until you have these acronyms memorized. You will need to refer to it in the remaining sessions.

QUALITY QUOTE

▶ *Leader's Note: Preach this confession with tenderness and sincerity.*

Even if I were utterly selfish and had no care for anything but my own happiness, I would choose, if God allowed, to be a soul winner, for never did I know perfect, overflowing, unutterable happiness of the purest and most ennobling order till I first heard of one who had sought and found a Savior through my means.
—*Charles Spurgeon*

The characters: Christian and Larry Lovelust
Scene setting: Christian and Larry are neighbors
who bump into each other at the post office.

Christian: "Hey, Larry. Good to see you
again."

Larry Lovelust: "Hey, Christian. What's
up?"

Christian: "Heaven. Do you still think
you will be going there?"

Larry Lovelust: "Sure. I told you, I'm as
good as any Christian."

Christian: "That wasn't the case the last time
we spoke. Have you forgotten how you
had broken all those Commandments
we went through? Are you still lusting after women?"

Larry Lovelust: "Absolutely. I love it. What you see as lust, I
see as pleasure. There's nothing wrong with looking at
a woman and thinking she's gorgeous."

Christian: "That's right. There's nothing wrong with that.
But remember what I told you. God says that there is
something wrong with *lusting* after her. He calls it
adultery of the heart."

Larry Lovelust: "So, how do you know the difference?"

Christian: "Your conscience. It will tell you when 'look'
changes to 'lust,' if you listen to it."

Larry Lovelust: "Well, like I said, it sure gives me a lot of
pleasure."

Christian: "Just because it gives you pleasure doesn't mean
it's right. Lots of things can give a person pleasure—
like arson, or an exciting bank robbery. It can be an
adrenaline rush for some people, with a big reward at

the end if you can outwit the police. Did you know that Jesus said if your eye causes you to sin, it would be better to pluck it out rather than let that sin take you to hell?"

Larry Lovelust: "I don't think God will send me to hell for just looking at women. Wow—look at that one. #!@&*!"

Christian: "Larry. Look at me for a minute. God won't send you to hell for just looking at women, but He will send you to hell for lusting after them, committing adultery with them in your heart. Listen, I hate to end our conversation like this, but I've got to go. Here's my card with my phone number on it. Give me a call the day you're going to die. Then we can talk more about eternity."

Larry Lovelust: "Huh? I don't know when I'm going to die."

Christian: "Exactly. Thanks for talking with me. Bye."

Be sensitive about when to end a conversation. If Larry wants to talk further, make sure you do so, but don't give him the message of God's forgiveness unless he begins to show some concern about his salvation. Lust is such a blinding and powerful sin, and a man will not want to let it go unless he becomes convinced that it's in his best interest to do so. Hell is a very good reason to do so.

Use the analogy of lust being like a sparkling stick of dynamite in a child's hand. He loves the sparkle and holds it with delight in front of his face, not realizing that it will kill him. Lust sparkles before the face of the unsaved, but it brings terrible destruction. The Bible says that "when desire has conceived, it gives birth to sin; and sin, when it is full-grown, brings forth death" (James 1:15). Try to awaken your hearers with the Law and turn them to the Savior with boldness and compassion.

▶ *Leader's Note: Stress the importance of completing the "Break Out of Your Comfort Zone" activities. Again, these homework assignments are critical for participants to learn and grow in this course. As they step out in obedience, God will be with them—and what could be more exciting than being used by God to impact someone's eternity?*

CLOSE IN PRAYER

Break Out of Your Comfort Zone

1. *At-Home Preparation:* Take out your Quick Reference Card and have a friend or family member test your memory. Once you are confident that you can remember what each letter signifies, go back to your mirror and give your friendly, "How are you doing?" Then swing to the subject of God. If you prefer, use an Ice Breaker and ask, "Did you get one of these?" Practice your routine. Say, "It's a gospel tract. What do you think happens after someone dies? Do you believe in heaven and hell?" Now go through WDJD and CRAFT. Keep doing it until you overcome any self-consciousness. Review the card a hundred times a day if you have to.

2. *Real-World Application:* Time for more sweaty palms. Last week, you were asked to give out tracts, and if you felt confident, to go ahead and hand them to people personally. Remember, you were to greet someone with a warm, "Good morning. How are you doing? Did you get one of these?" If the person asked you what it was, you said, "It's a gospel tract" or, "It has a gospel message on it. Please take the time to read it. Nice to meet you." You were then left with the option to stay and chat or to leave. More than likely, you left.

This week, making personal contact is not optional. Before the next session, we want you to hand a gospel tract to at least one non-

Words of Encouragement

On a recent crowded flight, as the last passenger boarded, she looked at her boarding pass and said, "I'm in the seat next to you." I thought, *Great, now I have no place to set my book down.* I am reading *The Way of the Master* and was heavily engrossed in Chapter 16, "How to Share Your Faith," when the realization hit me that I am supposed to do what the book recommends on an ongoing basis.

I am not a shy person, but when issues of such great importance as eternal life come up I get very still. As I sat in my seat I realized that this person next to me might not be safe from the judgment to come! That bothered me. I closed the book and asked God to give me courage. I saw that she was reading a book and noticed the word "God." I asked, "Good book?" She replied that it was, explaining that it was a fictional story about a man who writes obituaries for a newspaper.

Without thinking I asked, "What do you think will happen when you die?" She said, "That could take hours to answer and debate." From there I stuck to the "WDJD" approach. I walked her through "Would you consider yourself to be a good person," into several of the Ten Commandments, and then straight to Judgment Day. Tracy listened very carefully, asked questions, and slowly dropped her head as we spoke.

As we landed, she said she wanted to share what she had just heard with her husband. In addition, her mother-in-law and friend had been trying to get her into a Bible study for some time but had never explained "it" this way.

Fifteen minutes earlier I had sat in my tiny seat with perspiration running down my back, and now I was skipping through the terminal! —*Erik M.*

Christian, if you haven't done so yet. If you've already been doing this, then feel free to either leave or talk further, using the WDJD card for reference. (Be sure to always carry this card with you!)

We gave you a couple ideas of places to visit, but it's up to you to make this part of your lifestyle. *Wherever* you go, take tracts with you and hand them to people personally. And whatever you do, soak it in prayer, before and afterward. Remember the employee at the drive-through window, people in the coffee shop, the grocery store checker, the person in the elevator, the pizza delivery man . . . whoever. *You* make the opportunity.

So spend the next week being friendly and giving people Ice Breakers until it becomes second nature. You can do this!

For Deeper Study

1. Read 2 Samuel 12:1–14. Name the specific Commandments that David violated when he sinned with Bathsheba.

2. In 2 Samuel 11:27, the Bible tells us, "But the thing that David had done displeased the LORD." Using Romans 3:10–18,23, describe how the entire human race has "displeased the Lord."

3. God commissioned Nathan to reprove (rebuke) David. Read 2 Timothy 4:2 and explain the spirit in which we are commissioned to rebuke this world.

If you had been sent by God to rebuke David, would you have been fearful? If so, why?

4. How did Nathan begin his message? (See 2 Samuel 12:1–4.)

How did the king respond to this parable (verse 5)?

5. Explain what 2 Samuel 12:6 reveals about David. (See Exodus 22:1.)

6. Based on 2 Samuel 12:14 and Romans 2:23,24, what does hypocrisy do?

7. Notice the order of Nathan's message. He rebuked the king for the personal nature of his sin (verse 7), and told him that he had despised "the commandment of the LORD" (verse 9). Why didn't he just speak of God's love and mercy?

8. Read 2 Samuel 12:13. What effect did this message have on David? Why is this? (See Romans 7:13.)

9. Explain the order of the good news ("gospel") in 2 Samuel 12:13.

What does this teach us about how we should present the gospel?

LESSON 6
Answering the Top Ten Questions

► *Materials Needed: Additional Ice Breakers for each person. Participants will need to have their Quick Reference Cards with them.*

OPEN IN PRAYER

SHARE YOUR EXPERIENCES

Share the results of last week's "Break Out of Your Comfort Zone" assignment. Tell what happened when you stepped out of your comfort zone and handed tracts to people throughout your week. If you brought up the subject of God or heaven, was the person open? Were you confident about where to go with the conversation as a result of what you're learning in this course?

► *Leader's Note: Share with the group an interesting, funny, or exciting witnessing encounter that you've had recently.*

POINT TO PONDER

If you could ask God one question, face to face, what would it be? When Hugh Hefner was asked this, he replied, "Oh, I think the one question I'd really like to know is the question related to an afterlife. And the other question is the meaning of it all." We don't need to ask those questions because God has given His Word as a lamp to our feet and a light to our path. It illuminates the way so we know what's ahead of us.

The afterlife is no mystery, unless we make it a mystery by refusing to believe the truth of Scripture. Those who refuse to believe are left in ignorance and without any reason for existence. One well-known actor said that when he dies, his last words will be, "That was nice. I wonder what it was all about." What a tragedy! The ungodly have every reason to be utterly miserable both in this life and in the next.

As Christians, we don't need to ask about the purpose of life and what happens after death. If we were brave, we might ask how and when we will leave this life. Is that a frightening thought to you? Perhaps we should meditate on it, alarming though it may be. It would help us to be more careful when we cross the road or drive a car. But it would also help us to make sure that we inject eternity into the temporal. Thinking about life and its transient nature can help us to think about death and its eternal implications for the lost, and that's what matters most.

▶ *Leader's Note: Ask participants to get out their Quick Reference Cards, so you can all read the card aloud in unison. Lead the group in quickly reciting each phrase of WDJD and CRAFT.*

VIEW THE VIDEO **Answering the Top Ten Questions, Part 1 (19 minutes)**

▶ *Leader's Note: Pause after the first five questions and ask participants to form pairs. Have each partner select one of the following questions that he is most concerned about being asked in a witnessing encounter. Let them take turns asking their "nightmare" question and then listening as their partner gives the answer.*

Apply the Principles

These suggested answers are here for your convenience. You may have an answer that you feel is more effective. (For more detailed answers to these and many other questions, see *The Evidence Bible*.)

1. **"What about ignorant tribes in the deepest jungle who've never heard about Jesus?"**

   They will be fine on Judgment Day—*if* they have never lied, stolen, committed adultery (lusted), murdered (hated someone), etc. A person goes to hell not because he hasn't heard of Jesus, but because he's sinned against the Lord. "Sin is the transgression of the Law" (1 John 3:4, KJV). If those who ask this question are truly concerned about the ignorant tribes, they should get saved, become missionaries, and then take the good news of God's forgiveness in Christ to them.

2. **"My god is a god of love and forgiveness, and would never send me to hell."**

   This is an example of idolatry, where rather than making a god (an idol) with his hands, the person has created a god within his mind. He has reshaped God in his own image—a god with whom he feels comfortable. The God of the Bible is holy and just, and will by no means clear the guilty. God is merciful, however, and extends His forgiveness to all who repent and trust in His Son, Jesus Christ.

3. **"Why is there suffering? That proves there is no 'loving' God."**

   We live in a fallen creation. The Bible says, "Therefore, just as through one man sin entered the world, and death through sin, and thus death spread to all men, because all sinned" (Romans 5:12). Disease, suffering, and death entered the world as a result of man's sin. So we shouldn't blame God, but man. Rather than viewing suffering as an excuse to reject God, it should be seen as a very real reason to turn to Him. Suffering stands as a terrible testimony to the truth of the explanation given by the Word of God.

   It is a great mystery why God sometimes *allows* suffering (children with cancer, etc.), but despite the mystery, the Christian trusts God.

4. **"I'm already saved" (though evidence shows otherwise).**
   If a patient says he's healthy but his physician thinks he may have a disease, the doctor may ask if he has an appetite. A lack of appetite is a sign that something isn't right. Do the same: ask the person if he is reading the Bible daily. Someone who isn't right with God will avoid the Scriptures, because the Word of God brings conviction (knowledge of guilt). Someone once said of the Bible, "This Book will keep me from sin, or sin will keep me from this Book."

   Then ask if he thinks he is a good person. If he's a false convert, he will almost certainly say that he is, so take him through the Commandments, and warn him of the reality of Matthew 7:21–23.

5. **"I don't believe in God."**
   Just because we don't believe in something doesn't make it disappear. If a man walks down a freeway with an eighteen-wheeler heading toward him, and he says, "I don't believe in trucks," it doesn't change reality. The truck will kill him if he doesn't get out of its path.

   You can reason about God's existence by asking, "When you look at a building, how can you *know* there was a builder?" The build*ing* is proof that there was a build*er*. Use the same analogy with a painting and a painter, and then point to Romans 1:20 (creation proves there is a Creator). But don't stay long in the area of the intellect—address the conscience by using the Law. Your job isn't to convince the person that there is a God; according to Romans 1:20, he already knows that. Rather, it is to convince him that he needs the Savior, which the Moral Law will do.

VIEW THE VIDEO **Answering the Top Ten Questions, Part 2 (31 minutes)**

▶ *Leader's Note: Ask participants to form pairs again, with each person selecting one question from the following list and*

practicing the answer with his partner. Encourage partici-
pants to review these ten questions on their own at home, so
when they encounter them in witnessing, they will have a
confident response.

6. **"I don't believe the Bible is God's Word. It was written by men."**
   When you write a letter, who actually writes it—you or the pen? You write it; the pen is simply the instrument you use. God did the writing and He simply used men as instruments to communicate His thoughts to humanity (see 2 Timothy 3:16). To prove that God inspired these men, simply study Bible prophecy. Look at Matthew 24, Luke 21, 2 Timothy 3, and many other passages. The Bible's hundreds of fulfilled prophecies clearly show the fingerprint of God. (*The Evidence Bible* lists many prophecies, as well as scientific facts written in the Bible thousands of years before man discovered them.)

7. **"I confess my sins and say I'm sorry all the time."**
   This is a very common response by religious people (false converts, Roman Catholics, Muslims, etc.) when they are confronted with the fact that they have sinned against God. Use civil law as an example of how this makes no sense. A judge will not let a criminal go simply because he confesses to the crime, and says that he's sorry and won't do it again. Of course he should be sorry (because he has broken the law), and of course he shouldn't commit the crime again. Instead, a good judge will demand punishment—justice must be done. How much more will God demand that justice be done? He can release us from the requirements of the Law only because Someone took our punishment for us.

8. **"I've lied, but that doesn't make me a bad person."**
   A proud, self-righteous person will find it difficult to openly admit his sins. He may refuse to say, "I have lied, and that makes me a liar." Sin is like bad breath. It's easy to detect in others, but not so easy to detect in ourselves.

So turn it around by saying, "If *I* told a lie, what would that make me?" Most will quickly say, "A liar."

Don't be afraid to add that the Bible says that "lying lips are an abomination to the LORD" (Proverbs 12:22), and that even though we may not think there's anything wrong with lying, God says that *all* liars will have their part in the Lake of Fire (see Revelation 21:8). Always share this verse with concern in your voice. If the person still refuses to be honest, just move along to the next Commandment, as it is difficult to reason with an unreasonable person.

9. **"It's narrow-minded to believe that Christianity is the only way. There are many roads to God. So you're implying that Muslims, Buddhists, Jews, and Hindus are all going to hell?"**

It isn't Christians who originated this claim; it was Jesus Christ Himself who said, "I am the way, the truth, and the life. No one comes to the Father except through Me" (John 14:6). The best way to show that Jesus is the only way to God is to use the Law to strip the person of what he's trusting in—his self-righteousness. Let him see that he is under God's fearsome wrath. Show him that in trying to justify himself through his "good works," he is attempting to bribe the Judge of the Universe. He is heading for Eternal Judgment, and his only hope is the Savior. There is no other way a man can be justified.

Therein lies the great difference between Jesus Christ and all manmade religions. None of them can forgive sins—only Jesus can. He alone said, "The Son of Man has power on earth to forgive sins" (Matthew 9:6).

10. **What do you do if someone puts up a brick wall and says, "You take care of your life and I'll take care of mine. I don't agree with what you're saying."**

All you can do is present the truth in love. Tell the person that, worldwide, 150,000 people die every 24 hours, so he should get right with God today. Then in a firm but gentle tone, say, "If my eyes meet yours on the Day of Judgment and you are still in your sins, I'm free from your blood—because I have told you the truth." This sounds harsh, but which is harsher—that the person is offended by your frankness, or that he spends eternity in the Lake of Fire?

Don't be discouraged. If you have shared the truth, then God will be faithful to bring conviction of sin, in His time. Remember that when Paul reasoned with Felix about righteousness, self-control, and judgment, Felix just dismissed him (see Acts 24:25). Paul may have thought that he made no headway, but the Bible says that "Felix trembled" (KJV).

▶ *Leader's Note: As time allows, discuss the following questions.*

1. Do you think it's important to answer people's questions? Why or why not?

2. How can you avoid being sidetracked by someone's (rabbit trail) question?

3. What can you say if you don't know the answer to a question?

4. Read Luke 13:1–3. What can we learn about how Jesus answered questions?

QUALITY QUOTE

▶ *Leader's Note: This is a short one, so preach it twice, the second time with twice as much passion!*

Some wish to live within the sound of a chapel bell; I wish to run a rescue mission within a yard of hell.
—C. T. Studd

PREACHER'S PROGRESS

The characters: Christian and Dan Druff
Scene setting: Dan decides to argue with Christian as he's handing out Ice Breakers.

Dan Druff: "I think Christians are flakes!"

Christian: "Why's that?"

Dan Druff: "They are weak-minded people who need a crutch in life."

Christian: "You're right, if you define a parachute as a 'crutch' for someone jumping out of a plane."

Dan Druff: "Huh?"

Christian: "Don't you realize that you will someday have to pass through the door of death? That's when you'll need a Savior, or the 'crutch' you spoke about. When you die you will have to face a Moral Law that is far harsher than the law of gravity."

Dan Druff: "I don't believe in a Moral Law."

Christian: "That doesn't matter. If a man jumped off a ten-story building not believing in the law of gravity, he still has to face the consequences of his action, despite the fact that he doesn't believe in it ... Have you kept God's Law, the Ten Commandments? Have you ever told a lie?"

Dan Druff: "You're starting to get under my skin."

Christian: "I'm only telling you this because I care about you. God is going to judge with a fine-toothed comb on Judgment Day. He will judge right down to the thoughts and intents of your heart. In fact, the Bible says in Psalm 68:21 that 'God will wound the head of His enemies, the hairy scalp of the one who still goes on in his trespasses.' You need to repent today and put your faith in Jesus Christ."

CLOSE IN PRAYER

Break Out of Your Comfort Zone

1. *At-Home Preparation:* The Bible says to go into all the world and preach the gospel to every "creature." That may help you feel more comfortable about this suggestion. Make sure no one is around. Make doubly sure. Now witness to your dog. Go on. Do it. This is no more silly than talking to your mirror, and, again, it will help you get used to the sound of your voice. Just say, "Sit. Stay. I'm going to talk to you," and don't stop just because your pet cocks his head and looks at you like you're some sort of weirdo. Ask, "Did you get one of these? It's a gospel tract . . . Would you consider yourself to be a good dog? Have you ever stolen a bone?"

    If you don't have a dog, talk to your cat (if you are an animal lover, this is something you do all the time). If you don't have a pet, talk to your fern. The point is, practice, practice, practice. Proverbs 16:23 says, "The heart of the wise teaches his mouth, and adds learning to his lips." Practice whenever, wherever, and with whomever you can. You want to overcome your fears, and the way to do it is to go over this again and again until it becomes second nature.

2. *Real-World Application:* Forget the sweaty palms. This assignment will make your whole body break into a sweat. It's time to step out and see what God can do through you. You are going to get out of the house or leave your workplace during your lunch time and seek the lost. You are going to intentionally share the gospel with a sinner. So, go to the mall, visit a park, or just walk the streets until you see someone sitting on a bench or standing around—anyone you could engage in conversation. Ask God to direct you. Then go for it.

    Here's a refresher course: Be friendly and smile as you say, "Hello." If there's a warm response, ask, "Did you get one of these?" When the person takes it say, "It's a gospel tract. Have you had a Christian background?" Then ask, "What do you think happens after someone dies?" and so on. Take the person through the WDJD questions. Don't listen to your fears; instead, think of that person's eternal welfare. (You can do this!)

Go through at least three of the Commandments; if the person seems humbled, continue by following with the CRAFT acronym. Answer any questions the person may have, and encourage him to think further about these things. Don't forget to close with, "Thanks for talking with me. I really appreciate it."

If appropriate, offer your contact information; invite him to attend church with you (offer to take him); or give him information that will help him grow in his faith. Be sure to pray for the person to whom you had the privilege to speak.

For Deeper Study

1. The unsaved are governed by a "carnal" mind and walk "according to the flesh"(see Romans 8:5–8). Read Ephesians 4:17–19 and describe their condition.

Words of Encouragement

Dear Mr. Comfort,   May 2005
...Taking a cookie-cutter approach by repeating the same words over and over to different people makes you sound like a used car salesman laying down his 'spiel'...While that may work great with people sitting in a church who are halfway to the cross already, you lose your credibility among the ones who need saving the worst... —*Matthew G.*

Dear Mr. Comfort and Mr. Cameron,   September 2005
I can't believe it! I used your method of witnessing to one of my best friends, who is agnostic and a public defender for 30 years. I was nervous at first, but I kept focused on getting to the heart, and not the head. He still rejected the message, but at least I explained it to him in a way that makes common sense...I had been trying to witness to people for eight years, mostly "Christ crucified," but with limited success...

I told my friend I knew the Ten Commandments were God's Law (to which he agreed!) and I, as well as all mankind, had broken those Laws at one time or another. Anyway, I feel SO blessed to finally know an effective way to witness to people. You are truly doing God's work...Thank you so much for show-ing me how to witness to the "heart and not the head."
—*Matthew G., California*

P.S. You may have read an email I sent a few months back about my dislikes with your methods. I am very sorry, and have turned 180 degrees since. I thank God for imparting wisdom to you on how to witness properly, and I thank you for telling me, and the world.

2. Then read Galatians 5:19–21 and list the "works of the flesh"—the fruit of a carnal mind.

3. According to Titus 1:15, what has happened to the mind and the conscience of those who are unbelieving (carnal)?

4. What is the attitude of the carnal mind toward God (Romans 8:7)?

The Greek word for "enmity" used here is also used in Ephesians 2:15,16 and James 4:4, and is translated as "hatred" in Galatians 5:20. It is the opposite of the Greek word *agape* (love). It is this unbelieving, anti-God, Law-hating carnal mind that we're trying to reason with in appealing to a sinner's intellect. We must therefore, as soon as possible, find a place of harmony between the sinner's mind and God's Law. Where do we find that? (See Romans 2:15.)

5. How can we resurrect a defiled conscience and appeal to it?

6. Read Romans chapter 2, marking everywhere Paul mentions future punishment. Write comments on how and why he did so. Compare this to our typical witnessing methods today. Note where he mentions the Moral Law, and where he gives his hearers the "Good Test" by personally confronting them with the Commandments.

LESSON 7
Exposing the Myth of the Modern Message

▶ *Materials Needed: Participants will need to have their Quick Reference Cards with them.*
Leader's Note: Be prepared to announce a time and place for a group get-together this week to go fishing for men. Have plenty of additional tracts available for the "fishing trip."

OPEN IN PRAYER

SHARE YOUR EXPERIENCES

Discuss the results of last week's "Break Out of Your Comfort Zone" assignment. Who did you find to share the gospel with? Were you nervous? Were you able to remember the WDJD outline? What was the person's response? Share your experiences and pray for those who were witnessed to.

If you were too timid to witness to a person, did you witness to your dog? Was he offended? Did he receive your message or just throw you a bone? We hope you had fun with this!

POINT TO PONDER

Consider the late President Kennedy. One moment he was sitting in his limo, smiling and waving to adoring crowds. The next moment he was in eternity. A small piece of fast-moving metal sent him there in a split second. Imagine you were taken back to the time just before he stepped into the limo. You can't stop the assassination but you can talk to him for a moment about his eternal salvation. Are you so intimidated by his status that you would remain silent? Of course not! You know what will happen to him. You look beyond the presidency into eternity. You ignore your fears and look into his eyes. You see the frailty of his humanity, and think how in an instant of time he will be blasted into death.

All around us, people are smiling and waving at each other. They aren't thinking about their salvation. They can't see the invisible. They have no concept of the eternal. But you do. You know what awaits them. Death is snatching people every minute of every day. Within the next 24 hours, 150,000 people around the world will have stepped into eternity. Whatever you do, don't be intimidated into silence. Take the initiative. Look into eternity: "We do not look at the things which are seen, but at the things which are not seen. For the things which are seen are temporary, but the things which are not seen are eternal" (2 Corinthians 4:18).

▶ *Leader's Note: As you watch the video, ask participants to pay particular attention to the countenance of the girl being witnessed to as she is brought through the Ten Commandments.*

VIEW THE VIDEO **Exposing the Myth of the Modern Message (35 minutes)**

Apply the Principles

Have someone read Luke 16:19–31 out loud, then discuss the following:

1. Envision the rich man standing in your room, speaking to *you* at this moment. His clothes are smoking with heat; his terrified eyes are aflame. Imagine he is pleading with you to testify to his family. What would he have you say to them (verses 28, 30)? Did he want his family to hear about how to have a happy life, or how to avoid

the flames of hell? Do you think that you are as concerned as you should be about the *reality* of hell?

2. Have you ever felt that you couldn't witness to people who were already happy as they were? What was the cause of your dilemma?

▶ *Leader's Note: Ask participants to break into same-sex pairs for the following role-play, using their Quick Reference Cards as a guide.*

3. With your partner, take turns role-playing a witnessing encounter, with one person playing a Christian and the other playing a happy, healthy, successful (but unsaved) lawyer who loves his life just as it is.

▶ *Leader's Note: If you have a longer class time, you may want to discuss the following additional questions.*

4. Have you ever told people that God has a "wonderful plan" for their lives? What do you think the lost understand that to mean?

5. What negative things did Jesus say could be in store for those who trust in Him?

6. Explain what the Bible means by an "abundant" life.

7. According to Matthew 5:6, for what should sinners be "thirsting" when they come to Christ?

8. How can you "salt the oats" of the lost and make them thirst?

QUALITY QUOTE

▶ *Leader's Note: You may ruffle some feathers with this one, but people are going to hell... so preach every word of it!*

To try to win a soul to Christ by keeping that soul in ignorance of any truth, is contrary to the mind of the Spirit; and to endeavor to save men by mere claptrap, or excitement, or oratorical display, is as foolish as to hope to hold an angel with bird-line, or lure a star with music. The best attraction is the gospel in its purity. The weapon with

which the Lord conquers men is the truth as it is in Jesus. The gospel will be found equal to every emergency; an arrow which can pierce the hardest heart, a balm which will heal the deadliest wound. Preach it, and preach nothing else. Rely implicitly upon the old, old gospel. You need no other nets when you fish for men; those your Master has given you are strong enough for the great fishes, and have meshes fine enough to hold the little ones. Spread those nets and no others, and you need not fear the fulfillment of His Word, "I will make you fishers of men."
—*Charles Spurgeon*

PREACHER'S PROGRESS

The characters: Christian and Alec Smart
Scene setting: Christian is heckled by Alec as he's witnessing.

Alec Smart: "Hey, Christian, I've got one for you that I know you can't answer. Can God make a rock that's too heavy for Him to lift?"

Christian: "You know, you're pretty clever. Let me think about that. Now, could I ask *you* a question?"

Alec Smart: "Sure, go ahead."

Christian: "Would you consider yourself to be a good person?"

Alec Smart: "You bet."

Christian: "Okay, then. Have you ever told a lie?"

Alec Smart: "Never."

Christian: "Not once? Not a fib, white lie, half-truth, or exaggeration? You have always spoken the truth, the whole truth, and nothing but the truth, so help you God?"

Alec Smart: "Yep."

Christian: "Have you ever stolen anything?"

Alec Smart: "Not a thing."

Christian: "Not even a ballpoint pen? Maybe cheated on your taxes, brought home supplies from the office, taken things from your parents, or downloaded some illegal software?"

Alec Smart: "Nope. Never!"

Christian: "Wow. You know, Jesus said that if you look at a woman and lust after her, you've committed adultery already with her in your heart. Have you ever done that?"

Alec Smart: "No. Never!"

Christian: "You have a pure heart?"

Alec Smart: "Yep. Pure as the driven snow."

Christian: "Okay. Have you kept the First of the Ten Commandments?"

Alec Smart: "Sure."

Christian: "What is it?"

Alec Smart: "Huh?

Christian: "What is it—the First Commandment?"

Alec Smart: "Um...I don't know."

Christian: "It's to put God first in your life. Have you loved God with all of your heart, soul, mind, and strength?"

Alec Smart: "Sure have."

Christian: "Alec, God's Word says that no one seeks after God. None of us can say that we have kept the First Commandment. So one of you is lying—either you or God—and the Bible says that it's impossible for God to lie. So you've just broken the Ninth Commandment by lying to me, and the Scriptures warn that all liars will have their part in the Lake of Fire. Lying also shows that you don't fear God. Your "image" of Him is wrong; you've created a god in your imagination that doesn't mind lying. That's called idolatry. So you've also broken the Second Commandment. You are going to be in big trouble on Judgment Day."

Be prepared for people like this. They are so clever that they pride themselves in their ability to outwit Christians, so they can avoid any conviction of sin. Their "smart aleck" attitude isn't smart at all; it will get them into hell for eternity.

If the person is proud and self-righteous, don't be afraid to do what Jesus did with the self-righteous, rich young ruler. He let him walk away without hearing the gospel (see Mark 10:21–23). However, watch how the person responds when you ask, "Do you know what God did so you wouldn't have to end up in hell?" Some people will suddenly humble themselves and open their heart. So be open to the leading of the Holy Spirit each time you witness.

IMPORTANT GROUP ACTIVITY: **FIRST FISHING TRIP**

▶ *Leader's Note: Announce the group's first "fishing trip"—a prearranged opportunity for participants to share their faith and maybe even "catch a fish."*

Select a Friday or Saturday evening and meet at a place where lots of "fish" gather, such as an outdoor shopping center, movie theater, coffee house, ice cream store, etc. Make sure it is public property. Instruct participants to bring their own Ice Breakers, but provide plenty of extras just in case. Pray. Be organized. Split up into several small groups and do what you've learned in the class. For this first time, just spend an hour or so doing this so it isn't too intimidating.

It's very important to set a time to meet at the end of the evening to share your fishing stories and pray for those who were witnessed to. Sharing your successes, and any "failures," will energize participants and help to encourage everyone.

Break Out of Your Comfort Zone

1. *At-Home Preparation:* Do a search on the Internet for the word "evangelism" or "how to be saved." Check out the sites listed and find their gospel message. See if there is a sound biblical presentation of the gospel. Do they open up the Law as Jesus did, and warn of future punishment (is there reference to Judgment Day and hell)? Is there a mention of the cross, the resurrection, repentance, and faith? Is Jesus presented as the answer to life's problems or as the Savior from sin?

   If you don't have Internet access, watch Christian TV shows and analyze their gospel presentation (if there is one). Don't have a condescending or judgmental attitude, but determine to make sure you always put in what they leave out.

2. *Real-World Application:* Remember Jesus' words, "I will make you fishers of men"? This week your group will get together for just such an opportunity. If you haven't yet shared the gospel with someone, here's your chance to make it easier. Going together as a group will help you feel bolder, give you greater confidence, and provide accountability. If you feel

IF SOMEONE REPENTS AND TRUSTS CHRIST

If someone you witness to places his trust in Christ, it is essential that he be plugged into a local church (see Hebrews 10:25). We recommend giving the person a copy of *The Way of the Master New Testament*, which contains ten important principles for Christian growth—one of which is the fellowship of a local church. It also includes a very clear gospel message, as well as answers to questions they may have about God, Jesus, the Bible, hell, etc.

This book is ideal for leaving with someone who has trusted Christ, or is open to the gospel. In the front of the book, write your name and contact information. Make sure you get contact details from the person so that you can send information about the church closest to him (your church or one in his community). Then call the pastor of that fellowship and suggest that he contact the person to extend a personal invitation to his church.

Words of Encouragement

Thank you so much for the "Way of the Master" program. I have used it in my homeschool study group to show teenagers how they can evangelize their friends and families. I have also taken the principles and begun witnessing more accurately myself.

For years I have told friends and family about the wonderful life in Christ, only to feel a check in my heart because of all the trouble I've experienced, and was experiencing at the time, while I was telling them that they could have a better life if they only trusted Him. WOW! With the understanding about biblical evangelism that I've received from "The Way of the Master," it makes much more sense now. I now understand why I have so many trials; I no longer feel guilty or feel as though I am telling people a lie when talking to them about Jesus and their need for Him. I'm no longer frustrated about the trials and difficulties in my own life, where I once thought God didn't like me or I wasn't His child because life wasn't perfect, I now understand more about what is going on.

No longer do I believe that salvation is about improving one's life, although as a Christian we do have many benefits. It is about righteousness before a holy God and how His righteousness will demand wrath and judgment against the unrighteous on the day He has appointed. This is so freeing, so clear, and so wonderful. Thank you so much for this teaching! —*Joseph C., California* scared, this is normal. You can deal with your fears by saying, "I can do all things through Christ who gives me strength."

Carry your Quick Reference Card, and be friendly. Be compassionate. Be bold in your witness. People are going to hell, and you are there (with God's help) to lead them to the Savior. This is not a dress rehearsal; it's the real thing!

Of course, the goal is for everyone to join in this witnessing opportunity, but if you don't feel comfortable doing this, we strongly urge you to attend anyway and simply observe. If you know you should witness, and you want to learn, avoiding opportunities won't help you get there—it will only make it harder. So pray for boldness, and at least show up and watch the others. You will gain courage by seeing their experiences.

For Deeper Study

1. Explain what you think Paul meant in 1 Corinthians 11:1.

2. Read Jesus' words in Matthew 10:28. Despite being commanded to pursue the biblical example given by Jesus, it's not often that we hear preachers putting the fear of God in the hearts of their hearers. Why do you think so many shy away from doing that?

3. Explain this verse: "Faithful are the wounds of a friend, but the kisses of an enemy are deceitful" (Proverbs 27:6).

4. In John 5:45–47, Jesus told His proud hearers that Moses' writings accused them. Explain what you think He was saying. (See also Romans 2:12b.)

5. Jonathan Edwards said of the lost, "By a clear discovery of the connection between their sin and God's wrath, they are sensible of their danger of hell, of which many are in a measure sensible, who are wholly insensible of their desert of hell. The threatenings of the law make them afraid indeed, that God will punish sins." Put his statements into your own words.

6. Read Acts 9:1–9. It might seem that Paul's conversion simply came out of the blue on the road to Damascus. However, Scripture gives us insight into what brought him to the Savior. Read Romans 7:7–13. What helped Paul to see sin in its true light?

What specific Commandment had he violated?

What was Paul's view of sin without the Law?

What did the knowledge of the Law do for him?

What virtues are attributed to the Law?

7. According to verse 13, what else did the Law do for Paul?

8. Explain what the Law did for you before you came to Christ.

LESSON 8
Spreading Your Wings

▶ Materials Needed: The "Letters to God" written in Lesson 1; participants will need to have their Quick Reference Cards with them.
Leader's Note: Be prepared to announce a time and place for a group get-together this week to go fishing for men. Have plenty of additional tracts available for the "fishing trip."

OPEN IN PRAYER

SHARE YOUR EXPERIENCES

For the benefit of those who didn't attend, share the results of last week's "fishing trip." If you were afraid, did your fears prove to be true? Did people take the Ice Breakers you handed them? Were they open to talking with you? Did anyone repent and trust Christ that evening? Are you glad you went on the "fishing trip"? Would you recommend it to others? Discuss your experiences and pray again for those who were witnessed to that night.

POINT TO PONDER

The Bible tells us that eternal life is the free gift of God. It can come to humanity only as a gift; it can never be earned. Those who think that they merit salvation are deluded. They believe that God is their friend, a Helper in the sky whom they can call upon when they have problems.

However, the Bible teaches us the opposite. It says that, before we come to Christ, God is not our friend—He is actually our enemy. It also tells us that if we come to Him with a proud heart, He will resist us. It even says that our sins have made a separation between us and God so that He won't hear our prayers. Such thoughts are offensive to a godless world, but they are the truth. One way to explain our relationship to God is to consider civil law.

Imagine a man standing in court who has been charged with raping and murdering a young woman. He says to himself, "She was just a prostitute. I'm basically a good person, so the judge will no doubt be friendly toward me. I should be out of here by lunchtime." If he thinks like that, he's deluding himself, because he doesn't see the serious nature of his crime. When he hears the law's judgment for what he did, that should show him the seriousness of his offense.

Listen to sinners demean the serious nature of sin. Bearing false witness is simply telling fibs and "white lies." Theft is trivialized. Lust is "natural." Adultery is merely an "affair." They need to be made to tremble before God's Law, or they will never appreciate the beauty of the gospel. They need to hear the Law's judgment for their offenses—death and damnation—or they will not turn from their sin and trust in the Savior.

▶ *Leader's Note: Ask participants to get out their Quick Reference Cards and divide into pairs. Have them try to recite the WDJD and CRAFT phrases to each other without looking at the card even once. Invite a volunteer to stand and recite the entire card by memory.*

VIEW THE VIDEO Spreading Your Wings (33 minutes)

Apply the Principles

Have someone read the following article out loud to the group, then break into groups of three or four for discussion. The article was written by journalist Matthew Parris, who by his own confession is not a Christian.

The New Testament offers a picture of God, who does not sound at all vague. He has sent His Son to earth. He has distinct plans for each of us personally and can communicate directly with us. We are capable of forming a direct relationship, individually with Him, and are commanded to try. We are told that this can be done only through His Son. And we are offered the prospect of eternal life—an afterlife in happy, blissful or glorious circumstances if we live this life in a certain manner.

Friends, if I believed that, or even a tenth of that, how could I care which version of the prayer book is used? I would drop my job, sell my house, throw away all my possessions, leave my acquaintances and set out into the world burning with desire to know more and, when I had found more, to act upon it and tell others.

Far from being puzzled that the Mormons and Adventists should knock on the door, I am unable to understand how anyone who believed that which is written in the Bible could choose to spend their waking hours in any other endeavor.

1. Do you think that this man has a valid point? Why or why not?

2. In light of his claim—"I would drop my job, sell my house, throw away all my possessions, leave my acquaintances and set out into the world burning with desire to know more and, when I had found more, to act upon it and tell others"—do you think that *you* are doing all you can to reach this world with the gospel? If not, what changes would you like to make?

3. Do you know anyone who shares your concern for the lost, with whom you could go out as a witnessing partner? If so, why not set a date now and make it a regular part of your life? Just as Jesus sent people out two by two, making plans to go with a partner will provide encouragement and accountability, and will help you follow through when you might feel like backing out.

▶ Leader's Note: Hand out the "Letters to God" that participants wrote in Lesson 1.

It's time to read the letter that you wrote to God at the
beginning of this course. Take a minute to read it privately,
and then feel free to share with the group your thoughts
about what God has done in your life through this course.

QUALITY QUOTE

*▶ Leader's Note: Stand up and be heard. Your congregation is
waiting. Preach this one with all your might!*

I simply argue that the cross should be raised at the center
of the marketplace as well as on the steeple of the church. I
am recovering the claim that Jesus was not crucified in a
cathedral between two candles, but on a cross between two
thieves; on the town's garbage heap; at a crossroad, so cos-
mopolitan they had to write His title in Hebrew and Latin
and Greek . . . at the kind of a place where cynics talk smut,
and thieves curse, and soldiers gamble. Because that is
where He died. And that is what He died for. And that is
what He died about. That is where churchmen ought to be
and what churchmen ought to be about.
—George MacLeod

PREACHER'S PROGRESS

The characters: Christian and Darrell De'Seat
*Scene setting: Darrell overhears Christian witnessing to
someone.*

Darrell De' Seat: "Excuse me. I heard you talking to that
     person, and I don't think you have the right to judge
     her. The Bible says, 'Judge not, lest you be judged.'"

Christian: "I wasn't judging her. She told me that she was a
     liar, and I believed her."

Darrell De' Seat: "Well, I still don't think you have any
     right to say what you did. You embarrassed her. I'm a
     Christian, and what you did was wrong. Very wrong."

Christian: "Really? I'm only saying what the Bible says. It warns that all liars will have their part in the Lake of Fire. Aren't you at all concerned about where she'll spend eternity?"

Darrell De' Seat: "Yes. But that's not the way you should talk to people."

Christian: "What would you have told her?"

Darrell De' Seat: "That God loves her."

Christian: "May I ask you a question?"

Darrell De' Seat: "Sure."

Christian: "Would you consider yourself to be a good person?"

Darrell De' Seat: "Yes. I'm a very good person. Can't you tell?"

Christian: "Have you kept the Ten Commandments?"

Darrell De' Seat: "Yes, I have."

Christian: "You've never told a white lie, fib, half-truth, or an exaggeration?"

Darrell De' Seat: "Never."

Christian: "How could you say that you are a good person when the Bible says that there is none good—not one?"

Darrell De' Seat: "Now you're judging me! I think you are a !$@*! idiot and you shouldn't be ramming your beliefs down people's throats!"

Christian: "I'm not doing that. I'm simply warning people that God will judge the world in righteousness, and that they need the Savior."

Darrell De' Seat: "Get out of the Dark Ages! As long as these people believe in God and live a good life, they are okay."

Christian: "No, they're not. God says they must repent and trust Jesus Christ. If you're a Christian, you should know that."

Darrell De' Seat: "That's just your narrow-minded belief. So what if I've told a few lies in my life? I didn't hurt anybody. God's not going to throw me into hell just for some little white lie."

Christian: "Darrell, look at me. Nobody on the Day of Judgment will be guilty of just one little sin. The Bible says each of us have a multitude of sins. Sin isn't just doing what's bad, it's also failing to do what's good. Besides, God has seen your *thought* life as well as every secret deed you've done. *That's* what you'll have to give an account of on the Day of Judgment. *That's* why you need the Savior. It's not enough to just believe in God. You need to confess and forsake your sins. I hope you'll do that before it's too late. Thanks for listening to me."

Darrell De' Seat: "I've never heard it put that way before. You're welcome."

Don't be deceived into thinking that everyone who says he is a Christian is born of the Spirit. The Bible says that there are many tares among the wheat. One of the best ways to expose the non-Christian's deception is to take him through the "Good Test"; it's a powerful litmus test. Ask the person if he thinks that he is good.

If he is trusting in his own righteousness, pour on the heat. Any fear that arises in his heart because you mention his standing before God is a good thing. That fear will be nothing compared to the fear he will have if he faces God on Judgment Day without the Savior.

▶ *Leader's Note: Encourage everyone to attend this second fishing trip. It will be the final opportunity to get together in a real-life setting during this course. Announce the meeting time and place, and remind everyone to bring their own Ice Breakers. Encourage participants to not just watch others fish, but to cast their own line and try to pull in a big one!*

When you meet at your fishing hole, remember to pray before and after. Meet again at the end of the evening for a time of celebration. Go to a pizza place or ice cream parlor, and take time to share experiences and give praises to God for the glorious gospel—and for giving everyone the boldness to come to this event! This is an ideal time to hand out the Certificates of Completion for all who successfully attended the classes and put the teaching into practice. Remember, there is no greater joy than leading others to find eternal life!

CLOSE IN PRAYER

▶ *Leader's Note: After the prayer, encourage everyone to complete the final homework assignments, and to read the remaining section on "How to Witness" to cement in their minds the principles they've learned in this course.*

Invite participants to stay and talk with you about continuing their evangelism training through "The Way of the Master" Intermediate Training Course, or by leading their own group through the Basic Training Course.

Break Out of Your Comfort Zone

1. *At-Home Preparation:* Here's something to help you fight off sweaty palms. Have you ever watched a movie where a masked burglar crept through someone's house? The fact that you can't see his face produces fear, but somehow the fear dissipates the moment

the mask is ripped from his head and you see who he is. Today, we are going to unmask fear and see its real face.

Why are we afraid to give out a tract, or share the gospel with a family member, or talk to a stranger about his salvation? Isn't it because we fear rejection? What then is behind the mask of fear? It's the face of human pride. We don't want anyone to think badly of us. But look at God's attitude about pride: "Everyone who is proud in heart is an abomination to the LORD" (Proverbs 16:5). That sort of pride is a sin, so knowing what is under the mask will help to dissipate our fears. If we are humbled by being rejected, it's only our pride that is injured, and that's not a bad thing: "If you are reproached for the name of Christ, blessed are you...If anyone suffers as a Christian, let him not be ashamed..." (1 Peter 4:14,16).

Right now, spend a moment dealing with the sin of pride. Confess it and forsake it. Then in humility go and reach those who may be snatched into everlasting hell, while there is still time.

2. *Real-World Application:* Make it a priority to participate in the second "fishing trip" this week. We are to be doers of the Word, not hearers only, so it's crucial that you follow through—despite your fears—and learn to put these principles into practice. Pray for boldness, then do what you know you should. You will be glad you did—and so will the lost with whom you share eternal truths.

Determine with all your heart to continue to share your faith regularly after this course has ended. Force yourself to do this. Even if your greatest fear came upon you and you were beaten up (or just humiliated), Jesus said to rejoice and be exceedingly glad because even the prophets before you were persecuted. Think of what a child does when he's learning to walk. If he falls down, do you discourage him from trying again? No. You want him to grow up, so you encourage him to stand on his own feet, and to take more steps. So, if you fall down and get bruised, stand up, dust yourself off and take another step of faith.

We are not asking you to do something we haven't done. We know that a fall can be painful, but there's more at stake than your welfare, so ask God to give you such love for people that you won't think of yourself. Remember your Gethsemane experience, and

Words of Encouragement

On my way home one night, I stopped by my daytime "fishing hole." It was midnight. There were five teenage guys hanging out, so I did some night fishing. It was one of those conversations that was just so much of the Lord—just incredible.

After we finished talking, I went inside the place to get a drink, and came back out to find a group of three teenage guys. I gave them the Giant Money tract, not planning on witnessing because I was bushed. One of the guys said, "Hey, how about twenty bucks instead?"

I thought, *Oh boy, if that's not a lead-in from the Lord, I don't know what is.* So I said, "Twenty bucks? I'll give you twenty bucks if you can pass the Good Person test. Are you up for it?" They said, "Yeah, man, let's do it."

Thirty minutes later, these guys were totally transformed—they had gone from haughty, cocky teens to humbled lawbreakers admitting their need to make peace with God. I got home at 1:30 a.m. and felt as high as a kite. What a night! —*Larry L., Georgia* stop listening to the lies of the devil. Resist him steadfast in the faith, and say, "I can do all things through Christ who strengthens me."

Remind yourself that this is not a once-in-a-lifetime experience; this is the new you. See evangelism not as a church event, but as a lifestyle. Take the opportunities to impact people you see on a daily basis: the checker at the grocery store; the cashier at the dry cleaners; the gas station attendant; repairmen; your coworkers; your classmates; your teachers; security guards; friends; the baby-sitter; the mailman; your neighbors; your family members; etc.

You may want to begin a regular PIE night: Pizza, Intercession, and Evangelism (PIE). Meet with several others on a Friday night for a big slice of pizza, pray together for 15–20 minutes, then hit the streets or a mall to seek the lost.

Remember, you have enlisted as a faithful firefighter, and you have been studying how to rescue those who are about to die. Your life will never be the same. You are going to live for Christ. Work toward that goal with even more determination than you would put into making a marriage work. You don't want to lose your first love, and if you don't continually stoke the fire, it will go out. It's just a matter of time.

Here's some fuel for you to keep the flames burning for the lost:

- Read the Bible daily, without fail. Make it more important than your food.
- Maintain a regular daily prayer life.
- Keep your life free from all sin.
- Keep your eye on the cross.
- Meditate on the fate of the lost as a regular part of your prayer time.
- Always be ready to witness. Carry Ice Breakers (gospel tracts) and the Quick Reference Card with you at all times. Keep them in your wallet or purse.
- Find a local fishing hole and go there regularly with a buddy to fish for men.
- Spend more time with like-minded Christians who share your passion to reach the lost.

- Turn up the heat in your daily devotions—start reading *Morning and Evening* by Charles Spurgeon.
- Pray for wisdom.
- Let us be a continual source of encouragement to you through our free monthly e-newsletter. Go to www.WayoftheMaster.com to sign up.
- Take the next step in your learning by participating in "The Way of the Master" Intermediate Training Course or enrolling in the online School of Biblical Evangelism.

For Deeper Study

1. Read 2 Corinthians 12:9,10. How is God's strength made perfect?

2. Why did Paul boast in his weaknesses, or infirmities (see verse 9)?

3. Why should we take pleasure in our infirmities (verse 10)?

4. Write out a personal prayer to God, applying this principle to your weakness when it comes to speaking to the unsaved.

5. Read 1 Timothy 1:8–13. For whom is the Law made (verses 8–10)?

6. Who put Paul (and enabled him to be) in the ministry?

7. What did Jesus require of him (verse 12)?

How to Witness

This section summarizes much of the information from this course, to refresh your memory about what you've learned. There are also some additional helpful analogies and points to remember when witnessing. You may even want to extend this study to discuss the content of this section.

STARTING A WITNESSING ENCOUNTER

To get your feet wet in witnessing, an easy first step is learning to be friendly and talk with people. This may seem obvious, but make a habit of talking to your neighbors and coworkers regularly. Then practice being friendly with people at the park, at the gas station, or at the grocery store. Perhaps you already have an outgoing and friendly personality—that's great! If you tend to be a shy, introverted person, try to open up a little and start greeting people. A simple "Hi, how are you?" isn't difficult. Or say, "Nice day, isn't it? My name is so and so..." With a bit of practice, anyone can learn to be friendly. Most people respond warmly to warmth.

To share our faith effectively, we must let people know that we are not "weirdos" or religious fanatics. We must show them that we care, and we start by being friendly. A good friend (who is admittedly quite shy) mentioned that he and a buddy went to the park on a Saturday afternoon, just to practice being friendly to strangers. They had a great time, and had so much fun that they couldn't wait to get out the following weekend to take the next step.

After you have gained a measure of confidence in speaking to strangers, you can swing to the subject of spiritual things.

It's not wise to walk up to people and immediately assault them with talk about Jesus. They'll most likely think you're strange. Instead, start in the natural realm (everyday things) and then swing to the spiritual realm. That's what Jesus did (see John chapter 4). He began talking with the woman at the well about natural things, then He swung to the spiritual. You may want to talk about sports or the weather, and then perhaps use something in the news to transition to the subject of spiritual things.

Alternatively, you can simply ask if the person knows of a good church in the area. Or you can use a gospel tract. It doesn't matter how you do it, as long as you do it. Start in the natural realm so the person doesn't think you're a religious nut, and then make the transition any way you want. That will lead you directly into the conversation about God.

WDJD: THE FOUR STEPPINGSTONES

By following the WDJD outline from the Quick Reference Card, you can confidently lead *any* witnessing encounter. You will be in control of every conversation you have about your faith. Imagine—you will know exactly where you are in a conversation and you will know exactly where it is going. You don't have to study Greek or understand archaeology; you just have to follow the four "steppingstones" to reach your goal. You can say goodbye to your fears.

There is no doubt that the first point is the most difficult to ask. Once you've brought up the subject of spiritual things, it becomes much easier. Here are the four steppingstones in the WDJD acronym.

W: Would you consider yourself to be a good person?

You will be surprised to find that people are not offended by this question. If they say "No" (highly unlikely), ask them what they mean. Remember, you are asking people about their favorite subject —themselves. Most likely you'll find that they are kidding or that they've done something in their life that they feel badly about.

Otherwise, expect individuals to respond, "I'm a pretty good person" or "I'm a *really* good person." This reveals their pride and their self-righteousness. At this point you are ready to use the Law (the Ten Commandments) to humble them . . . the way Jesus did. Now move to the next steppingstone.

D: Do you think you have kept the Ten Commandments?

Some will say yes, others will say no. Regardless, you simply continue by saying, "Let's take a look at a few and see. Have you ever told a lie?" Some will admit to lying; others will say they have told only "white lies"; a few will claim they have never lied even once. Gently press the issue: "Do you mean to say that you have never told anyone a lie to deceive them? Even once?" Usually they will say something like, "Maybe when I was a kid." Ask, "What does that make you?" They will hesitate to say, but get them to admit, "A liar."

People do not get angry with this approach; instead, they become sober. They may declare, "I don't believe in the Bible." Simply continue on your course. If they argue about the Bible, say, "I know you don't believe it. I am simply sharing with you what the Bible says. Okay? Let's keep going."

Continue going through the Commandments. You may want to ask about stealing next, then the Seventh Commandment, then the Third. Here is an example of how to go through each one:

#9 We covered "lying" above.

#8 "Have you ever stolen anything?" Many will claim that they haven't. "Have you ever taken anything that did not belong to you, regardless of its value—anything? Even when you were younger? Be honest before God." Some will try to trivialize theft by saying that they stole when they were a child. Ask, "What does that make you?" and press them to say, "A thief."

#7 "Have you ever committed adultery?" Again, most will say no. Add, "Jesus said, 'Whoever looks at a woman to lust for her has already committed adultery with her in his heart.' Have you ever looked at someone with lust?"

#3 "Have you ever taken the Lord's name in vain?" Some will try to wiggle out of this, but just press a little: "You mean you have never used God's name casually, or to express anger?" Most will admit to this one. Then gently explain, "So instead of using a four-letter filth word to express disgust, you have taken the name of the One who gave you life and everything that is precious to you, and you have dragged it through the mud. People don't even use Saddam Hussein's name to curse, and you have used Almighty God's name? That is called 'blasphemy,' and God promises that He will not hold anyone guiltless who takes His name in vain."

Note: You should be noticing something at this point. The individual will either grow quiet (his "mouth may be stopped" by the Law, Roman 3:19) or will be getting agitated. If the person seems to recognize his guilt, you may want to say at this point, "By your own admission, you're a lying thief, a blasphemer, and an adulterer at heart, and we've only looked at four of the Ten Commandments." If he is still trying to defend himself ("I'm not a bad person"), go through a few more Commandments.

#6 "Have you ever murdered anyone?" Obviously, most will say that they haven't. Point out, "Jesus said that if you merely call your brother a fool, you are in danger of judgment, and the Bible says if you've ever hated anyone, you are a murderer in God's eyes. God does not simply judge actions, He knows the intentions of the heart."

#1 "Have you always put God first in your life?" Most will admit that they haven't. "God says that He is supposed to be the primary love of our life. In fact, Jesus said that our love for God should be so great that our love for our parents, kids, friends, even our own lives should seem like hatred by comparison."

#2 "Have you ever made an idol, a god to suit yourself?" People will usually say that they haven't. "Have you pursued money more than God? Then you have made money an idol. Have you given work more attention than God? Then work is an idol. If you think, 'God is loving and wouldn't send me to hell,' you are correct; your god wouldn't send anyone to hell, because your god doesn't exist. He is a figment of your imagination. You've created a god in your own mind that you're more comfortable with, and that is called 'idolatry.' It's the oldest sin in the Book and God warns us that idolaters will not inherit the Kingdom of God."

#5 "Have you always honored your parents, treating them in a way that is pleasing to God?"

#10 "Have you ever coveted, or jealously desired something that did not belong to you? Covetousness reveals a lack of gratitude for what God has already given you."

#4 "Have you kept the Sabbath holy? God requires one day out of seven for you to rest and acknowledge Him, and you have failed to give Him what He has demanded. How many times have you neglected to bow your head before your meal and thank Him for the food He has provided? How many thousands of times do you think you've just greedily dug in without thanking your Provider?"

J—Judgment: If God judges you by the Ten Commandments on the Day of Judgment, will you be *innocent* or *guilty?*

If the individual has not yet begun to show signs of conviction, he will more than likely start now. Most people will sense where you are going with the conversation and say, "Innocent." But they must understand and confess their guilt if they are ever to come to Jesus (see Proverbs 28:13). The following will help them do that. Use this as a guide in directing the conversation and dealing with common responses. Again, this is not a script for what to say; feel free to use your own words.

Them: "I'm a pretty good person."

You: "You just told me that you broke God's Commandments, the Moral Law. By your own admission, you're a lying thief, an adulterer at heart, a murderer, and a blasphemer. Think about it. Will you be innocent or guilty?"

Them: "But I haven't done those things for a long time."

You: "Imagine saying that in a court of law. 'Judge, I know I am guilty but it has been years.' He won't ignore your crime. He will see that justice is served and will punish you no matter how much time has elapsed. The courts punish war criminals from decades ago, and God doesn't forget sin no matter how long ago a person did it. Do you think you will be innocent or guilty?"

Them: "But I have done more good than bad."

You: "Again, think of a court of law. If you have broken the law, you are guilty. It doesn't matter how many good deeds you've done when you are being tried for your crime. You have broken God's Law. Will you be innocent or guilty?"

Them: "But that's man's law. God is different."

You: "You're right. God can never be bribed. And His standards are much higher than a human judge's. He loves justice and has promised that He will punish not only murderers and rapists, but also liars, thieves, adulterers, and blasphemers. You are in big trouble, aren't you?"

Often, people become awakened (aware of their sin), but not alarmed. In other words, they understand they have broken God's Law, but it seems that they just don't care. Your goal is to see them alarmed, because they should be—they are in great danger. This line of reasoning can help:

> Let's imagine that a computer chip has been placed behind your ear, and it records everything that runs through your mind for a whole week: every secret thought, every deed, and every word that comes out of your mouth. Then all of your friends and family are called together and all of your thoughts are displayed on a big screen for them to see. How would that make you feel? Embarrassed? Ashamed? That is just what will happen on the day when God requires you to give an account for everything you've said and done for your whole life. All of your secret thoughts will be laid before Him. You are in big trouble.

It's wonderful to get a confession of guilt, but if the person simply won't be honest and admit his guilt, at some point you may have to help him. Say, "If you would just be honest, you know you will be guilty before God. Besides, that is what the Bible says and if you claim to be innocent, you are calling God a liar."

D—Destiny: Will you go to heaven or hell?

Gently ask, "Do you think you will go to heaven or hell?" People won't be offended because you are simply asking a question, rather than telling them where they're going. Some will say, "Hell," but most will say, "Heaven." If they think they are going to heaven, you can use this analogy:

Consider this. You are standing in a court of law, guilty of a serious crime. There is a $100,000 fine. The judge says, "You are guilty. Anything to say before I pass sentence?" You answer, "Yes, Judge. I'm sorry for what I have done. Please forgive me." Can a good judge let you go simply because you say that you are sorry, or that you won't do it again? Of course not. There is a $100,000 fine that must be paid. However, if someone pays the fine for you, can the judge then let you go? Yes; once the fine has been paid, your debt to the law has been satisfied and the judge can set you free.

In the same way, each of us is guilty before God, and He will not let us go simply because we say that we're sorry or that we won't do it again. Of course, we should be sorry, and we shouldn't do it again. However, the fine for our crime must still be paid.

If the person responds by saying that this is man's justice, and that God's ways are different, agree with him. Say that God's justice is far harsher than man's justice, and that His standards are infinitely higher.

Don't be afraid to tell people that if they die in their sins, the Bible makes it clear that they will go to hell. Ask, "Does that concern you?"

If they say that it doesn't concern them, or if you sense they are not humbled and don't recognize their need of God's forgiveness, it's very helpful to describe what hell is like until they show signs of concern. According to the Bible, hell is a place of eternal, conscious torment, where "the worm dies not, and the fire is not quenched"; there is "weeping and gnashing of teeth," "everlasting punishment," "shame and everlasting contempt," and "eternal fire . . . the blackness of darkness for ever." Tell them that you don't want them to go to hell, and God doesn't want them to go to hell. Plead with them. If they do not seem concerned, it may be that they are just hiding it.

Don't feel pressured to give the Good News to a proud, self-righteous (rebellious, cussing, arrogant) sinner who is not willing to admit his guilt before God. Remember, Jesus didn't give the gospel to the rich, young ruler, because he needed the Law to humble him first. You will have to watch and listen carefully because humility is not always obvious.

If the person admits that it does concern him, only at that point should you go to the gospel. If you are able to detect humility (the person is no longer justifying and defending himself), or his responses indicate that he has been humbled, you now have the glorious pleasure of sharing the Good News.

SHARING THE GOSPEL

The Good News

Here's a good way to begin sharing the gospel: "God provided a way for you to be forgiven. The question is, how do you access this forgiveness?" Take the time to explain this thoroughly: "God loves you so much that He sent His only Son to suffer and die in your place, taking your punishment for you so that you could live. It's this simple: you broke the Law and Jesus paid your fine. Then Jesus rose from the dead and defeated death. If you will repent—turn away from sin—and place your trust in Jesus Christ alone as your Savior, God will forgive you and grant you everlasting life. He will change you from the inside out, and make you a new person in Christ."

This is the time to *magnify the love of God* to the sinner. Now you have the green light—go for it! Don't hold back: show the amazing length, width, depth, and height of God's love for the person as a sinner. This is when you pull out John 3:16. God offers complete forgiveness of sin and the gift of everlasting life *freely* to those who will surrender everything to Him through faith in Jesus Christ.

Ask the individual if he understands what you have told him. If he is willing to confess and turn from his sins and trust the Savior for his eternal salvation, encourage him to pray and ask God to forgive him.

The Prayer

Should we pray the traditional sinner's prayer with someone who we think is willing to turn from sin and trust in Christ? Perhaps this will shed some light on the subject: If someone you know committed adultery, would you lead him back to his wife and say, "Repeat after me: 'I am really sorry. I should not have slept with that woman'"? More than likely you wouldn't. If someone says he wants to pray right then and there, encourage him to do so. You might like to say, "You can pray right now. Confess your sins and turn from them, and then tell God you are placing your trust in Jesus as the Lord and Savior of your life. Surrender your heart to Him. After you've prayed, I'll pray for you."

Then make sure the person has a Bible (get him one if necessary), and encourage him to read it daily and obey what he reads. Also, encourage him to get into a Bible-believing, Christ-centered church.

If the person doesn't ask you to pray with him, let him go on his way, but encourage him to think deeply about your conversation and to get his heart right with the Lord as soon as possible. You can then leave him in the hands of a faithful God, who will continue to speak to him through His Holy Spirit and bring him to genuine repentance in His time.

For a thorough treatment on why we should be very careful about hastily leading someone in a prayer for salvation, visit our website at www.wayofthemaster.com and check out "How to Botch an Altar Call" (under Tools / Resources).

Inoculated "Almost-Christians"

If you are dealing with an inoculated churchgoer who knows a few Bible verses (such as John 3:16), you probably have the toughest encounter of all. The person may answer all the questions correctly, but you know he doesn't live like a Christian should. Here are some questions that might reveal his level of understanding:

1. "Are you born again?" If he says he isn't, remind him that Jesus said a man must be born again to enter the Kingdom of God (John 3:5).

2. "When was the last time you read your Bible?" If he says it's been a long time, express your concern by asking, "What would you think if you sent love letters to your wife and she never took the time to read them? You would start to suspect that maybe she isn't very interested in you. God sent you sixty-six letters and you rarely read them. What should He conclude about your love for Him?"

Encourage the person to examine himself to see if he is in the faith (2 Corinthians 13:5). If there are no signs that he has been born again, if there is no fruit in his life to indicate that he is a child of God, ask,

"Would you consider yourself to be a good person?" If he says yes, something is radically wrong, and you should take him through the Law.

The Place of Apologetics

While apologetics (defense of the faith) play an important part in evangelism, it's vital to realize that they have a limited function in reaching the lost. If we confine our witness to arguing about the existence of God, the inspiration of Scripture, the age of the earth, etc., we are like a man who goes fishing with bait, but no hook. While he may attract the fish, they will end up fat and happy...and they will get away. The function of bait is to attract the fish and disguise the hook. When the fish come around, the fisherman pulls the hook into the jaw, and catches his fish. Apologetics are the bait, and the hook is God's Law. It is the Law that appeals to a man's conscience and brings the knowledge of sin.

Hell-fire Preaching

It's important to realize that when we talk about the Law and the reality of hell and Judgment Day, we aren't referring to "hell-fire preaching." Hell-fire preaching will produce fear-filled converts. Using God's Law will produce tear-filled converts. Those who hear only the message of hell, without the Law to make it reasonable, come to Christ because they want to escape the fires of hell. But in their heart, they think God is harsh and unjust, because the Law hasn't been used to show them the exceedingly sinful nature of sin. They don't see that they *deserve* eternal damnation, that hell is their just dessert. They don't understand mercy or grace, and therefore lack gratitude to God for the cross—and gratitude is the prime motivation for evangelism. There will be no zeal in the heart of a false convert to evangelize.

However, those who hear and understand the Law come to Christ knowing that they have sinned against heaven. They know that God's eye is in every place beholding the evil and the good, and that God has seen darkness as though it were pure light. He's seen their thought life. If on the Day of Judgment God in His holiness exposed all the secret sins of their hearts, if He revealed all the evidence of their guilt, He could pick them up as an unclean thing and cast them into hell *and do what is just and right*. But instead of giving them justice, He has given them mercy and grace. He's demonstrated His love toward them in that while they were yet sinners, Christ died for them. They therefore fall on their knees before that bloodstained cross and say, "Oh, God, if You did that for me, I'll do anything for You. I delight to do Your will, oh, my God. Your law is written on my heart."

HELPFUL ANALOGIES TO USE IN WITNESSING

If the person to whom you are witnessing seems to be having trouble understanding a spiritual truth, you may find these analogies helpful. (See *The Evidence Bible* for these and many others.)

You Don't Just "Believe" in a Parachute

A churchgoer may need help understanding the difference between just "believing in Jesus" and being "born again." Say, "If you and I were on an airplane and we knew we were about to crash, and I had my parachute on and you didn't, what is the most loving thing I could do for you? It would be to tell you to put on your parachute! If you told me you already believed in the parachute under your seat, but you didn't put it on, I'd plead with you to strap it on right away —because I know what will happen to you if you jump without the parachute. Simply believing in the parachute will not help you; you must put it on for it to do you any good.

"That's what the Bible says you must do with Jesus. It's not enough to simply 'believe' in Jesus (even the demons 'believe'); you must 'put on the Lord Jesus Christ' in order to be saved. You do that by repenting and placing your trust in Jesus as Lord and Savior. It's called being born again."

The Good Judge

A person may say that, although he's sinned against God, he will go to heaven anyway. This is usually because he thinks that God is "good," and that He will therefore overlook sin in his case. Point out that if a judge in a criminal case has a guilty murderer standing before him, the judge, if he is a good man, can't just let him go. He must ensure that the guilty man is punished.

Say, "If the judge just let him go, he'd be a corrupt judge and should himself be brought to justice. If he is a good judge, he will do everything in his power to see that justice is served. Likewise, if God is good, He must (by nature) punish murderers, rapists, thieves, liars, adulterers, fornicators, and those who have lived in rebellion to His Law and to the inner light that God has given to every man in the conscience."

But God is also rich in mercy, not wanting anyone to perish. He demonstrated His love for us on the cross. Tell the person, "We broke God's Law and Jesus paid our fine. If you will repent and trust in Jesus, God will forgive your sins and dismiss your case."

The Value of a Soul

If the person you are witnessing to doesn't seem to understand the seriousness of immediately getting right before God, try this: "Would you sell one of your eyes for a million dollars? What about both of them for ten million? Of course you wouldn't—no one in his right mind would—because your eyes are precious to you. If you think about it, your eyes are merely the windows of your soul (your life). Your life 'looks' out of your eyes. If your eyes are precious to you, how much more should you value your life?

"Jesus said, 'If your eye causes you to sin, pluck it out. It is better for you to enter the Kingdom of God with one eye, rather than having two eyes, to be cast into hell fire.' Jesus also said, 'What will it profit a man if he gains the whole world, and loses his own soul?' There is nothing more important than your own soul and where you will spend eternity."

Right in His Own Eyes

Many people don't think about the consequences of their actions and don't realize that they themselves are responsible. Consider the way dogs cross the road. A dog will wander onto a freeway oblivious to the danger. His tail wags as he steps between cars without a second thought. Cars swerve. Tires squeal. The noise is deafening as vehicles smash into each other. The sleepy dog stops wagging his tail for a moment and looks at the pile of smoldering, broken cars on the freeway. His expression betrays his thoughts. His bone-burying brain doesn't realize for one moment that he is responsible for the disaster.

When man wanders onto the freeway of sin, his tail wags with delight. He thinks that this is what he was made for. His thoughts of any repercussions for his actions are shallow. His mind wanders into lust, then predictably he wanders onto the path of adultery. Suddenly a disaster sits before him. His marriage is shattered, his reputation is ruined, his children are twisted and scarred. But like the dumb dog, he doesn't realize for one moment that he is solely responsible for his sin. What he has done is right in his own eyes. This is why the perfect Law of God needs to be arrayed before his darkened eyes—to show him that his way is not right in the eyes of a perfect God.

IMPORTANT POINTS TO REMEMBER IN WITNESSING

Communication consists of more than our words. When it comes to sharing our faith, there are certain aspects that we often overlook. The following are points to keep in mind.

Tone of Voice

It is imperative that we ask God for the right spirit, tone, and attitude in a witnessing encounter. We don't want to come across like a "know-it-all," or as arrogant. Our attitude should be humble compassion mixed with a deep concern. Be resolute, but gentle. Don't be smug with your arguments. We're called to speak with gentleness and respect, like compassionate doctors with a cure. We should never become angry, or even raise our voice. We have the freedom to speak very boldly, if the hearer senses that we are coming from a place of love and concern.

Gestures

Don't point your finger at someone in a judgmental way. Be careful even of your body language. Don't stand above people if you can help it; sit down beside them. Don't have a smug grin on your face as though you are winning an argument, or fold your arms as though you are scolding a child. Remember, above all, that you are only a fellow sinner saved by God's grace, pleading with others to come to the Savior.

Your Testimony and the Law

If you choose to give your testimony when witnessing, remember to weave in the Law. Here's how *not* to testify: "Before I knew Jesus, I was sad and unfulfilled. I tried everything but it just didn't make me happy. Then I gave my heart to Jesus and I have been so happy ever since." Remember, that will introduce a false motive. Instead, say something like this:

> Years ago I lived for myself. Then I looked at the Ten Commandments and I realized that I had broken God's Law. I began to understand that He saw me as a liar, and that all liars will have their place in the Lake of Fire. I realized that I had used His holy name as a filth word, and that He doesn't hold people guiltless who take His name in vain. [Go through all Ten Commandments if you are able to.] That is when I realized that I was going to be in big trouble on Judgment Day, and that I deserved to go to hell. I certainly didn't want to go to hell—that's a place I never want to experience. Then I heard that Jesus did something truly amazing: two thousand years ago, He was brutally whipped and beaten, and nailed to a cross. He willingly shed His blood and died in my place so that I could be forgiven. I broke the Law and Jesus paid my fine—He took my punishment for me.
>
> When I heard that, I dropped to my knees, confessed my sins to God, and gave my life to Jesus Christ. Ever since then, I have been reading the Bible because I want to know more and more about the One who loves me so much that He died for me. Now I know that I have eternal life, and will be found "not guilty" on the Day of Judgment—not because I'm a good person, but simply because of God's mercy.

This testimony is only an example, showing how to properly present the issues. Obviously, you need to tailor your story to reflect your personal experience. It is important to remember the principle of law before grace, and to use the Moral Law to bring the knowledge of sin before sharing the gospel.

Loving Our Neighbors

The greatest way to love our neighbors is to share the gospel with them. But neighbors are like family—we don't want to offend them unnecessarily, because we have to live with them. We need to be rich in good works toward all men, but especially our neighbors. The Bible reveals that good works are a legitimate means of evangelism. Jesus said, "Let your light so shine before men, that they may see your good works and glorify your Father in heaven" (Matthew 5:16). It is God's will that "by doing good you may put to silence the ignorance of foolish men" (1 Peter 2:15). Sinners may disagree with what you believe, but seeing your good works makes them think, "I don't believe what he believes, but he sure does. He certainly is sincere in his faith."

A friendly wave, a gift for no reason, fresh-baked goods, etc., can pave the way for evangelism. Offer to mow your neighbors' lawn or help do some painting. Volunteer to pick up their mail and newspapers while they're on vacation. Compliment them on their landscaping and ask for gardening tips. Invite them over for a barbecue or dessert. Pray for an opportunity to share the gospel, and be prepared for it when it comes.

Practice

Keep your Quick Reference Card with you at all times, and practice going through WDJD and CRAFT as often as needed until you have them memorized. Find a friend and role-play. You had to practice almost everything else in life—walking, writing, reading, riding a bike, driving a car. Evangelism is no different. Once you have these memorized and begin putting them into practice, you will start an incredible evangelistic adventure. You will be amazed that the responses of those you speak to will be very predictable. In no time at all, sharing your faith will become second nature to you. What's more, God will be with you every step of the way.

HELPFUL VERSES TO USE WHEN WITNESSING

Exodus 20:1–17 (the Ten Commandments)

Psalm 51 (as an example of a prayer of repentance)

Isaiah 53:5,6

Ezekiel 18:4

Matthew 5:27,28

Matthew 7:21

Matthew 12:36

Luke 13:3

Luke 16:15

John 3:3

John 3:16

John 3:18

John 3:36

John 14:6

John 14:21

Acts 4:12

Acts 17:30,31

Romans 2:5,6

Romans 5:8

1 Corinthians 6:9,10

Colossians 1:20–22

Hebrews 9:27

1 John 1:9,10

Leader's Helps

This section will give you an overview of all the materials and preparation that are needed in this course. Facilitating the study doesn't require any special training, just a love for the Lord and for the lost. If you can simply follow the content given in the study guide, provide a few materials to participants, and plan two "fishing trips," you are well qualified to lead this course with confidence. Have a positive attitude and expect God to do great things through your group!

MATERIALS AT A GLANCE
(Items you will need to provide for each participant)

Lesson 1:   • Study Guide
            • Paper, pen, and envelope

Lesson 3:   • 5 Ice Breakers (gospel tracts)

Lesson 4:   • Quick Reference Card
            • 10 Ice Breakers

Lesson 5:   • 15 Ice Breakers

PRINTABLE ITEMS

To help you inform others in your church about the Basic Training Course and encourage them to participate, we have included two promotional items on a CD for you to print in the desired quantity.

Provided are a 5.5" × 8.5" bulletin insert (printed two-up) and an 11" × 17" poster. These color files can also be printed in black and white.

Also provided is a printable Certificate of Completion, to give to those who successfully complete the course and put its principles into practice.

TRACTS

As you will discover, Ice Breakers are very valuable in sharing the gospel and are used heavily during this study. The course includes 300 tracts to get you started, but you will need to order more. How soon you run out depends on your group size. For example, with a group of 10, each person would receive 30 Ice Breakers, which we hope they will have handed out by the end of Lesson 5.

We have suggested the number of tracts that participants give out in Lessons 3, 4, and 5. Rather than having people feel overwhelmed, we want each person to be able to accomplish these minimal goals to increase their confidence. Once they begin leaving tracts and handing them to people, participants should find their tract use increasing with each lesson.

We recommend that each week you give participants the tracts needed for each lesson, so you can gauge the group's activity and provide encouragement to those who need it. If some are hesitant to give out tracts, don't overload them with more each week, leading them to feel discouraged that they can't keep up. If others are zealous to give tracts to everyone they meet, be sure they have an ample supply!

Make sure additional tracts are available beginning in Lesson 6, and especially for the two "fishing trips" in Lessons 7 and 8.

Tracts can be ordered at www.WayoftheMaster.com. To save on shipping, you could order a large quantity and make them available for participants to purchase. Or your church may want to purchase these for your use as part of its outreach effort.

In fact, we've found that most participants are interested in several resources mentioned in the videos, so you may find it helpful to set up a resource table during the course. You or your church can order a variety of the most popular items and make them available for purchase. In addition to Ice Breakers, we suggest *Evidence Bibles*, *The Way of the Master* book, *The Way of the Master New Testament*, *How to Know God Exists*, and CDs such as "Two-in-One," "What Hollywood Believes," and "God Doesn't Believe in Atheists."

Before the Study Begins

Order one Study Guide and one Quick Reference Card for each participant.

Lesson 1

- Study Guide for each participant
- Paper, pen, and envelope for each participant

Collect the "Letters to God" that participants have written and set them aside for safekeeping. You will need to return them to the participants in Lesson 8.

Review the "Break Out of Your Comfort Zone" and "For Deeper Study" assignments with the group. Remind participants of the importance of completing the homework before the next lesson.

Lesson 3

- 5 Ice Breakers (gospel tracts) for each participant

So that participants can role-play using different Ice Breakers, provide at least one of each of the three tracts included with the course. If you have ordered additional tracts to give participants a greater variety, let them practice with those also. You can view tracts at www.WayoftheMaster.com; you may want to get the Sample Pack (one of each tract) to help you pick your favorites.

Provide at least 5 tracts for each person to begin using this week for the homework assignment. The IQ Test and the $1 Million Bill are good to start with because they can simply be left somewhere, but the Curved Illusion is used to begin a conversation. Save that Ice Breaker for Lesson 5 or 6.

Lesson 4

- One Quick Reference Card and 10 Ice Breakers for each participant

Encourage participants to keep the card in their wallet so they'll always have it with them. Remind them that they'll need their card in each of the remaining sessions.

Lesson 5

- 15 Ice Breakers for each participant

Lesson 6

- Additional Ice Breakers for each participant

Lesson 7

Select a time and place for the first "fishing trip," and make any necessary arrangements. Choose a Friday or Saturday evening and meet at a place where lots of "fish" gather, such as an outdoor shopping center, movie theater, coffee house, ice cream store, etc. Make sure it is public property.

Instruct participants to bring their own Ice Breakers, but provide plenty of extras just in case. Pray. Be organized. Split up into several small groups and do what you've learned in the class. For this first time, just spend an hour or so doing this so it isn't too intimidating.

It's very important to set a time to meet at the end of the evening for "debriefing"—sharing your successes, and any "failures," will energize participants and help to encourage everyone. Be sure to pray for those who were witnessed to.

Lesson 8

- The "Letters to God" that participants wrote in Lesson 1

Select a time and place for the second "fishing trip," and make any necessary arrangements. Instruct participants to bring their own Ice Breakers, but provide plenty of extras just in case.

When you meet at your fishing hole, remember to pray before and after. Meet again at the end of the evening for a time of celebration. Go to a pizza place or ice cream parlor, and take time to share experiences and give praises to God for the glorious gospel —and for giving everyone the boldness to come to this event!

- Certificates of Completion

Your celebration event is an ideal time to hand out the Certificates of Completion for all who successfully attended the classes and put the teaching into practice. Remember, there is no greater joy than leading others to find eternal life!

Additional Resources

For additional insight and tips on sharing your faith the way Jesus did, we invite you to sign up for our free weekly e-newsletter, which contains ministry updates, articles by Kirk Cameron and Ray Comfort, witnessing stories, notices of new Ice Breakers (tracts), special offers, etc. We want to be your witnessing resource center and a continual source of encouragement, inspiration, and blessing to you. Go to www.LivingWaters.com and click on "Free Weekly Update."

You can also gain further insights by watching "The Way of the Master" television program (www.WayoftheMaster.com), as well as "Living Waters University" witnessing clips on YouTube. For hands-on training, we encourage you to check out our Ambassador Academy, "Transformed" and "Deeper" conferences.

Don't miss these other helpful publications:

- *The Way of the Master*
- *What Did Jesus Do?*
- *How to Bring Your Children to Christ…& Keep Them There*
- *The Way of the Master for Kids*
- *How to Know God Exists*
- *The Way of the Master New Testament*
- *World Religions in a Nutshell*
- *Spurgeon Gold*
- *Out of the Comfort Zone*

For a catalog of books, tracts, CDs, and DVDs by Ray Comfort and Kirk Cameron, visit www.livingwaters.com, call 877-496-8688, or write to: Living Waters Publications, P. O. Box 1172, Bellflower, CA 90706.

For a list of Spanish resources, please see www.AguasVivientes.com.

Intermediate Training Course

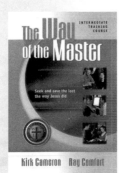

This eight-session DVD course adds critical framework to your foundation. It will teach you how to avoid the devastating pitfalls of producing false conversions. You will learn how to prove the existence of hell, both through the Scriptures and through reason, and what to do when things go wrong. Discover how to witness to a family member or to someone who is gay, how to recognize subtle satanic doctrines, how to refute the theory of evolution (join Kirk and Ray as they take an orangutan to lunch), and how to prove the existence of God.

School of Biblical Evangelism

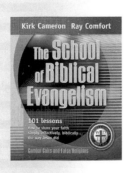

Join more than 9,000 students from around the world in the School of Biblical Evangelism, and learn how to witness and defend the faith.

With 101 lessons on subjects ranging from basic Christian doctrines to knowing our enemy, from false conversions to proving the deity of Jesus, you will be well-equipped to answer questions as you witness to anyone. This study course will help you to prove the authenticity of the Bible, provide ample evidence for creation, refute the claims of evolution, understand the beliefs of those in cults and other religions, and know how to reach both friends and strangers with the gospel.

Join online at **www.biblicalevangelism.com**
or call **800-437-1893**
to obtain the entire course in book form

The Evidence Bible

"*The Evidence Bible* is specially designed to reinforce the faith of our times by offering hard evidence and scientific proof for the thinking mind."

—Dr. D. James Kennedy

The Evidence Bible, based on more than two decades of research, has been commended by Josh McDowell, Franklin Graham, Dr. Woodrow Kroll, and many other Christian leaders.

- Learn how to show the absurdity of evolution.

- See from Scripture how to prove God's existence without the use of faith.

- Discover how to prove the authenticity of the Bible through prophecy.

- See how the Bible is full of eye-opening scientific and medical facts.

- Read fascinating quotes from Darwin, Einstein, Newton, and other well-known scientists.

- Learn how to share your faith with your family, neighbors, and coworkers, as well as Muslims, Mormons, Jehovah's Witnesses, etc.

- Glean evangelistic wisdom from Charles Spurgeon, John Wesley, George Whitefield, D. L. Moody, John MacArthur, and many others.

- Discover answers to 100 common objections to Christianity.

Find out how to answer questions such as: Where did Cain get his wife? Why is there suffering? Why are there "contradictions" in the Bible? . . . and much more!